Heart Whispers

Stories of Women Listening to Their Innate Wisdom
and Designing a Life They Love

Compiled By
Sue Urda
Kathy Fyler

Powerful You! PUBLISHING
Sharing Wisdom ~ Shining Light

Heart Whispers
Stories of Women Listening to Their Innate Wisdom and Designing a Life They Love

Copyright © 2023

All rights reserved. No part of this book may be reproduced by any mechanical, photographic, or electronic process, or in the form of a phonographic recording; nor may it be stored in a retrieval system, transmitted or otherwise copied for public or private use–other than for "fair use" as brief quotations embodied in articles and reviews–without prior written permission of the publisher.

The authors of this book do not dispense medical advice or prescribe the use of any technique as a form of treatment for physical, emotional, or medical problems without the advice of a physician, either directly or indirectly. Nor is this book intended to provide personalized legal, accounting, financial, or investment advice. Readers are encouraged to seek the counsel of competent professionals with regards to such matters. The intent of the authors is to provide general information to individuals who are taking positive steps in their lives for emotional and spiritual well-being. If you use any of the information in this book for yourself, which is your constitutional right, the authors and the publisher assume no responsibility for your actions.

Published by: Powerful You! Inc. USA
powerfulyoupublishing.com

Library of Congress Control Number: 2023908317

Sue Urda and Kathy Fyler – First Edition

ISBN: 978-1-959348-16-0

First Edition June 2023
Self-Help/Personal Growth

Dedication

*This book is dedicated to all
who wish to live life
as the fullest expression
of their innate knowing.*

Table of Contents

Foreword	vii
Introduction	xi
CHAPTER 1 ~ Love After Loss: One Woman's Journey to Finding Inner Peace *Erin O'Connor*	1
CHAPTER 2 ~ Great Enough *Dr. Sabrina Franconeri*	9
CHAPTER 3 ~ Your Heart Will Lead You Home: How I Left the Dark Room and Rebuilt My Life *Lin Moctezuma*	17
CHAPTER 4 ~ Just Say YES! *Carrie Clark*	25
CHAPTER 5 ~ Leading with a Courageous Heart: Divinely Aligned Messages in Action *Dr. Lara May*	33
CHAPTER 6 ~ Nurturing Synergy Through the Union of Spirit and Science *Sharon Montes, M.D.*	39
CHAPTER 7 ~ The Journey to Happiness and All Things Like It *Nicole C. Carey*	47
CHAPTER 8 ~ Fall Seven Times and Stand Up Eight Times *Tsuki Imie*	55
CHAPTER 9 ~ Turning Points: Ordinary Days Can Lead to Major Life Shifts *Sue Campanella*	63
CHAPTER 10 ~ Say YES and Hang On! *Amy Budd*	71

CHAPTER 11 ~ When a Whisper Becomes a Roar *Beverly Akhurst*	79
CHAPTER 12 ~ Becoming Empowered *Virginia Hunter Sampson*	87
CHAPTER 13 ~ Nurture Your Soul and Start Living Whole *Sarah Hauth*	95
CHAPTER 14 ~ A Message from Green Tara *Kathy Sipple*	103
CHAPTER 15 ~ True Love *Heather Dare*	111
CHAPTER 16 ~ Beyond the Fear *Debbie Weiss*	119
CHAPTER 17 ~ Concussion: 0	Heart: 1: How a Bang On The Head Led Me To My True Calling *Melissa Griffiths*	127
CHAPTER 18 ~ My Healing Journey: The Path to My Spiritual Life Purpose *Pamela Emmert*	135
CHAPTER 19 ~ A Spiritual Scavenger Hunt *Millie America*	143
CHAPTER 20 ~ Journey of the Heart *Linda Stansberry*	151
About the Authors	159
Acknowledgments & Gratitude	161
About Sue Urda and Kathy Fyler	162
About Carol Collins	163
Powerful You! Publishing	164
Collaboration Books	165

Foreword

Every once in a while—it is something that we like to say in advance of a nugget of wisdom. But, every once in a while in the way that you use that phrase you become who you are. Sometimes that reflection helps you to hold steady in who you have become or who you are trying to become. Lives are meant to be lived fully, not full to the brim with activities and with awareness of what everyone else has, what everyone else is doing, how everyone else has recovered and that they have recovered. We want you to live life full-ly, joyful-ly, kindful-ly, loveful-ly, friendful-ly—happy in other words.

When you have so much happy and all things like it then you can be guided by us who are participating, although you know it not, in your life.

When people reflect on their lives they do so because they can do nothing else in that moment or in that phase. It is generally a shock to the system because the inner mind is not reflecting, it is not remembering, it is reliving. It is reliving the moment in time that is stored in the memory of you.

Inside the part of you that contains life experience, those memories are still vibrant. Truly they are not memories at all. They are more like a video recording. The sight, the sound, the smell, the sensation, the topic, the scenario, the background are within the video of the mind. The video contains one more thing, the emotional contribution that went with the memory—the emotional density that you were feeling as well as the emotional density that everyone in that mind's eye recording captured. Those emotional

Heart Whispers

elements ARE. Everything is captured.

Sometimes you do not know why your life has taken the turn that it has. It is always because of emotional density that was erroneously stored in your memory. Your now, it is a mirror of then, in all of your reflective moments.

The pages of this book are vibrant with, "I recovered, I learned it, I am prideful, and I am willing to share my story in hopes that some or all is helpful to another." We love that. It alters your traumatic memories because you find yourself saying, "I am better, now." When you reflect and add "I recovered from that, I moved away from that, I stepped forward and I'm happier because of it" you alter that which was even more.

As you read the stories of others that have chosen to share something about themselves, be joyful, and their recovery and their learning increases because of your joy and your knowledge of their accomplishment.

Do consider positive reflection as an activity worth doing and worth sharing. All of you have stories. All of you have been living lives. All of you have emotional density. There are ways to clean it up. Heart Whispers is a healthy book. It is a good read. Let yourself be guided on what to read from it. Open the book with your eyes closed, perhaps. Bookmark the table of contents and open to that, perhaps and allow your eyes to be shown which story to read next. Where the book opens there is something for you even if it opens part way through a story. Do that first each time and your trust in guidance amplifies, your knowing of it amplifies the inner acknowledgement that guidance is available to you.

The authors are all unique yet are similar. They contribute positivity to the world. The publishers contribute exclusively positivity to the world. They have chosen that as their mission. It is nice when people do things like that for other people. Savor each page, dog ear, and write in the margins. Joyful comments increase your own learning and your own recovery and your own

Foreword

gap between that which you are recovering from.

We love people and we love lives and we love short stories and we love who you are becoming. We love and we love and we love. Period. Learn to do the same—just love for the sake of loving. Love on others then yourself because sometimes it is easier to focus on others. So do that! By and by you will experience an interesting effect—when you love on others and then yourself you have received love twice. All is well.

We love you so much,

Jeshua Collective of Teachers
As channeled by Carol Collins

Introduction

Sharing your story is risky.
Some will be moved, some dismayed,
and some won't understand.
When you choose to share from your heart,
despite what others think,
you risk moving mountains.

Storytelling is an art and a calling. It is also a gift, a contribution, a love letter to the world. This book and these authors are no exception.

Most authors came forth already open and willing to go to the depths of their personal journeys. They knew their stories could change the hearts, minds, and even the lives of readers. Others came to their stories 'kicking and screaming'—even though, of course, they decided to open their hearts. Interestingly, those who fought themselves the hardest along the way to painstakingly bare their souls are now content in the knowledge that they stepped forward from their inner selves and unleashed their hearts for the higher good, knowing that if one soul is touched, the fear and deep inner work of writing is well worth it.

The simple act of stepping into the work and allowing oneself to be vulnerable provides healing for the heart and spirit.

And so, herein lie the hearts and souls of 20 incredible women. Some of them had no idea that they were writers until the title of this book and the opportunity to collaborate called to them. They were drawn by a compelling force to open to the truth of themselves. Now, on the other side of the writing process, they will tell you that they have put forth not only their hearts and souls, they also reveal the essence of some very significant aspects of their lives.

When you are called to share your story, there's nothing that will stop you; not fear, not angst, not lack of confidence, not the monkey mind, and certainly not the voice of anyone else. The call, the pull, is so great that it must be answered. It's as if the choice is not really yours…although of course, the calling is your inner voice and it must be affirmatively answered.

In talking with each of the authors, we know the overwhelming reason and decision to write their story was to help someone else who is searching for answers, someone who needs encouragement and a light shone on the path before them. Many tell of the ecstasy or agony of their transformation or the happy story of how things can work out beautifully no matter the starting point. Others share secrets that they have guarded for many years and, for the first time, emerge from their silence because of the opening, opportunity, and healing that comes along with it.

What they all discovered is that an energetic transformation occurs when one puts pen to paper (or fingers to the keypad) with the intent to reveal her truth. As you read each story in this book, you will find yourself feeling the very core of the emotion of each author, whether she is speaking of creating or expanding a business, healing from some sort of tragedy, trauma, or abuse in her life, opening to her inborn gifts and talents, or she is still finding her way by tuning in and listening to her heart.

Each transformation is unique and holds its own gifts.

Heart Whispers. If you are drawn to the title of this book, you are undoubtedly on your own journey of awakening to a more conscious way of being. You are ready to step more fully into your

Introduction

power and, in fact, by picking up this book, you're already doing it. You have already leaped ahead toward your destination and, as you flip through the pages and read the words, you will catapult yourself even further along this path. Why? Because we are all connected, and your desire and willingness cannot help but move you forward. The only question is; *will you go forth with ease?*

**Are you ready and willing
to listen to the whispers of your heart?**

Our wish for you is that you commit to yourself to be aware of your calling, your purpose, your joy. Delve into your heart, listen to your inner voice, and answer the calling of your soul's purpose—however great or quiet, wherever it shows up, and whatever or whoever is the bearer. Be faithful to your desire to live in and from your heart space. As you do this, you will find your life to be more filled with love, more guided by Spirit, and more consciously aligned with your heart whispers.

With deep gratitude and love,
Sue Urda & Kathy Fyler

CHAPTER 1

Love After Loss

One Woman's Journey to Finding Inner Peace

Erin O'Connor

When I was nineteen, my father told me that forty was a good age to get married. At the time, I laughed in his face and thought I'd *never* be that old. Turns out, I *was*. I was thirty-nine when I got married—well, technically, I was thirty-eight because Billy and I were married twice. Our legal wedding happened in our living room on a cold Wednesday evening in December. Billy and I were dressed in jeans, and a lovely justice of the peace named Rose married us before Billy's parents and our three dogs, squeaky toys and all. That was a formality, however. Our REAL wedding took place six months later (and after my birthday) in the Dominican Republic. I say our "real" wedding because that's when I wore my wedding dress.

It was a simple yet elegant affair at a beautiful resort in Punta Cana, with my cousin officiating. I wasn't born with the bride gene, so a big fancy wedding never appealed to me. I was more excited about celebrating our love—and making sure everyone else did as well. The entire resort knew I was getting married because in the days leading up to our wedding, I announced it to anyone who would listen. Each day new guests arrived, and by June 29, 2014 we were surrounded by forty-six of our closest friends and family.

On the big day, the wedding coordinator escorted me to the front entrance of the hotel, then went to get my dad, who would walk me down to meet Billy at the garden gazebo. As I stood in my wedding dress, holding my gorgeous bouquet of tropical flowers, a bus of hotel guests pulled up beside me, and I shouted to them, "I'm getting married!" (as if they couldn't tell). I was on cloud nine.

When my dad arrived, we glided through the hotel lobby to the sounds of "Somewhere Over the Rainbow" and hotel guests clapping and cheering. As we rounded the corner to the gazebo, I looked over at my dad and asked him, "Did you think this would ever happen?" His response: a flat-out "No." I had a history of dating shady characters. I kissed many frogs before meeting my prince. But I knew from the moment I met Billy that he was different. He was kind and loving, and he oozed integrity. He taught me everything I needed to know about being in a healthy relationship, and, for the first time, I felt completely safe and loved.

Billy and I were married for two and a half wonderful years. Then, on September 4, 2016, Billy went to work and never came home. An accident on the job had robbed the world of this loving soul and left me a forty-one-year-old widow.

I'd never considered myself a "spiritual" person, but when a friend suggested I see a medium to connect with Billy, I jumped at the chance. Exactly sixteen days after he crossed over to the other side, I found myself sitting in the tiny back room of a metaphysical healing center an hour from my house. Some will say that was way too soon, but I say to hell with them. Within minutes this woman, whom I had never met, started sharing intimate details about my life with Billy. She knew how he died. She knew I laid my head on his chest in the hospital that day, and she even knew of his love for Budweiser. I laughed, cried, and everything in between until suddenly, there was a knock on the door. The shop's owner let us know our time was up. There was so much more I wanted to hear

Chapter 1
Love After Loss

and needed to hear, but that sixty-minute session gave me a glimmer of hope. Billy was gone from my physical world but not gone from my life. I just needed to learn how to speak his new language, the language of signs.

My first sign came in the bottle of Bogle Cabernet a friend's husband brought over one evening. He popped the cork, and there it was, a fancy letter B. You may read this and think it's just a cork, but I knew instantly it was a sign from Billy because my nickname for him was "B." And from that moment on, I seemed to see Bs everywhere.

A few months after Billy's passing, I was invited to attend a meditation retreat in New York. There were so many things about this that scared me. First and foremost, I was very new to meditation and the retreat was five days, three of them silent. Second, the drive was a little over three hours, and long drives made me nervous. And last, I would be going alone. I hated going to new places and events alone. Hoping Billy would guide me in the right direction, I asked him to show me a B sign if I was meant to attend the retreat. Less than an hour later, a friend and I drove to Whole Foods. On the way, I told him all about the retreat, my nervousness around it, and how I had asked for a sign. The words had no sooner come out of my mouth when we saw a giant B on the jeep in front of us. It had a Boston Bruins tire cover! That was the first time I realized I could ask Billy for guidance, and he would answer me. His guidance that day changed the trajectory of my career.

Learning to love Billy across the veil came easily. Our connection was stronger than ever, honestly. He always had a great sense of humor, and even that shines through the signs he sends me. Have you ever seen a dog throw up in the shape of a heart? I have, and it was right at my feet. All I could do was laugh and say, "Thank you, Billy."

Billy found a way to intervene in my love life too. In the days after his passing, one of his closest friends, T, asked me if he could have one of Billy's Red Sox jerseys. I had no use for the jersey, and I knew it was special to T, so I eagerly agreed to pass it along to him. Despite our sadness, we laughed because Billy had a way of putting things in places that only he knew about. Finding it would take a bit of time.

T and Billy had grown up together, and though I didn't know T well (he moved to Utah for work shortly after Billy and I started dating), I could always tell he was a gentle soul with a big heart. In fact, T was Billy's only male friend who checked in on me after he died. It started with sporadic, random texts like "What's on the menu tonight?" to which I'd reply, "A handful of chips and a slice of cheese." Those text messages were the start of a deep connection that neither of us expected.

I found the jersey just in time for Christmas and T's return. While he was home visiting family, we bonded over Billy. Once-a-month text messages turned into daily messages. I started to look forward to hearing from him. I felt both joy and guilt. Thank God for my therapist, who helped me understand that feeling joy after a loss was good. She reminded me that our purpose here is to love, be loved, and experience joy. So, whenever he returned home from Utah, we would get together, eat pizza, and reminisce about Billy. The more I got to know T, the more I enjoyed his company, and before long, I knew I had "more than friends" feelings for him. I could tell he felt the same way because one night while sitting at my kitchen counter, he looked at me like Billy had. He looked at me like I was the only woman on the planet.

Less than a year after Billy died, T and I shared our first kiss in my kitchen on what we called a "Pizza Friday" night. I felt that from my head all the way down to my toes. It was the kind of kiss you hear about only in the movies. The intensity left me reeling.

The following day I went for a spa day with a girlfriend. The

Chapter 1
Love After Loss

second I got in her car, I blurted out, "T and I kissed last night!" I felt like a giddy teenager in high school who finally kissed the boy she had been crushing on. We talked the entire ride about the kiss, my feelings, his feelings, and of course, the guilt. Widow guilt is no joke. It can honestly ruin the best moments if you choose to let it. Luckily for me, the guilt was short-lived. When we arrived at the spa, I got out of the car and stopped dead in my tracks when I saw a giant heart-shaped puddle! At that moment, I knew Billy approved, and to this day I believe he may even have orchestrated the whole thing.

T and I fell in love, and within the year, he moved back to his home, which was around the corner from me. I could hardly believe it—some people go their entire lives without finding true love and I was fortunate to find it twice. Again, with my therapist's support, I learned a vital lesson about myself: I had allowed myself to love again because I was taught very well HOW to love. Billy had given me that gift, and even though being in a new relationship scared me I knew I was well-equipped to handle it. When someone you love dies, it can either expand or close your heart. I felt like my heart grew like the Grinch's heart at the end of the cartoon. I swear it doubled in size.

My relationship with T was beautiful and complicated. In the beginning, many people frowned upon our union. Some thought I was moving too fast, and others shamed T for making a move on "Billy's wife." Despite their opinions, we embraced the challenges with grace.

Our love for each other was undeniable, but just as some suspected, I never truly faced my grief because we fell in love so soon after I lost Billy. Instead, my relationship with T masked it. On the surface, I was deeply in love again, but deep down, I had not fully processed Billy's death. In fact, it sometimes felt like there were three of us in the relationship. Finally, after four years,

T and I decided to end it—not because we didn't love each other but because we couldn't figure out how to work as partners. I didn't realize it then, but I'd placed many unrealistic expectations on T. I expected him to pick up exactly where Billy left off and that was unfair to us both.

The breakup felt like I was reliving Billy's death all over again, but the pain was double this time. I was grieving not one but two extraordinary men whom I loved very deeply. My nervous system reacted as if T had died, and the trauma of losing Billy resurfaced. I couldn't eat or sleep and felt lost and alone once again. Only this time, I didn't have T to help pick up the pieces of my broken heart. I needed to learn how to pick up the pieces on my own. I needed to take a deep dive and do some serious inner work.

I read books, listened to podcasts, watched webinars, and worked with two therapists. The journey was long and painful, but along the way, I learned that the root of my pain was abandonment, which stemmed from childhood. I'd never felt 'enough' on my own and therefore spent most of my life seeking out others to fill that void in me. I poured my love into all my relationships because I feared being left alone, but ironically, I was abandoning myself.

The little girl inside of me so desperately wanted to be loved—but not by just anyone. She wanted and needed to be loved by *me*. Losing Billy and T was the catalyst for learning to love myself. My grief became my most prominent teacher, and I am forever grateful for it.

Now, at forty-eight, I can fully embrace the woman I am today. I AM enough by myself. I know Billy will continue to be my North Star guiding my way, and T will forever be in my heart. This may seem strange, but I feel honored to have loved and lost both Billy and T. Losing both men brought me home to me, and there's no place I'd rather be.

Chapter 1
Love After Loss

ABOUT THE AUTHOR: Erin O'Connor is a Mindful Schools Certified Mindfulness Instructor and the founder of Happy Humans Mindfulness, where she empowers children, parents, teachers, and educators with mindfulness skills for a better life. Erin has twenty-one years of teaching experience at the kindergarten and first-grade levels. Erin also currently teaches mindfulness at Endicott College in Beverly, Massachusetts. Through her mindfulness course, she helps graduate students learn and apply mindfulness concepts and practices to improve their daily, academic, and professional lives.

Erin O'Connor
Happy Humans Mindfulness
happyhumansmindfulness.com
erin@happyhumansmindfulness.com
978-771-7705

CHAPTER 2

Great Enough

Dr. Sabrina Franconeri

"Am I good enough?" Women ask themselves this question too much. As a born perfectionist, I have been trying to answer that question for over forty years. As early as I can remember, I knew I was going to earn a doctorate and be successful. I was incredibly sure of what I wanted but allowed bullying, judgment, and my own insecurities to change my course. That question crept up more than necessary and I missed out on valuable experiences because of it.

Like many women, I tended to downplay my accomplishments, strengths, and securities. My journey forced me to notice patterns, speak up when I thought it was impossible to do so, and tolerate far less than I ever would have imagined. My heart has served as an amazing compass along the way as I searched for an answer to that haunting question.

The Kickball "Incident"

As a child, I was described as "gutsy" and "feisty "with exceptionally high self-esteem. I was so confident that when my grandmother's house, packed with our large family on Christmas Day, felt like it was one hundred and ten degrees, I had no shame in stripping down to my underwear and T-shirt. I was so secure that during a family picnic, I sprayed my father's Italian aunts with a water toy called the Fun Fountain when I was told it was time to stop playing. It was predicted that I was going to be a challenge once I went to school!

All of this changed when I had to play kickball in first grade. While the other kids kicked and ran like Olympic athletes, I was terrible. So terrible that I quickly earned the reputation of being last picked in gym class and was teased repeatedly for my lack of athletic ability. Although I had friends and fun in elementary school, I felt different. Having experienced how quickly people could judge me (and over a stupid thing like kickball) caused me to constantly question myself. The girl who ran freely in her underwear and sprayed people with the Fun Fountain vanished. While I earned decent grades and went on to have typical adolescent experiences, I still credit kickball for planting the seed of the constant question, "Am I good enough?" It percolated through high school and college.

Charmin Toilet Paper

I found myself in an emotionally abusive relationship in my second year of college. I allowed him to take over my choices in wardrobe, hair, food, and even sleeping position. This impacted my relationships with people that I loved. It takes two to tango and I know that this relationship caused me to do and say things that I'm not proud of to this day. Constantly concerned that I would be labeled a failure if I stayed single, the relationship grew to be more serious and we became engaged. I ignored my family and friends who told me I was selling myself short. I had a beautiful wedding, but started questioning my decision right away.

Now every aspect of my life was controlled. I dropped out of graduate school because he said the program was not the right fit for me and surrendered my monthly paychecks, having every penny I spent scrutinized. I left my teaching job because he said I wasn't earning enough, a move that would set me back professionally. Hoping for a compliment, I traded my edgy style for white sweaters and plain clothing because he liked them. I wanted presents, flowers,

Chapter 2
Great Enough

and attention because I thought these gestures meant he loved me. I was looking for physical evidence and constantly asked myself, "Am I good enough to be in this marriage?"

I didn't recognize myself anymore. This was beyond the bullying I'd been subjected to on the kickball field. I had an inkling that the only way I was going to make this better was to get out. Was I really confident enough to swallow my pride, follow my heart, and recognize that this was the best thing for me? Was I good enough to get a divorce at twenty-seven and start over?

I was not emotionally mature enough in first grade to highlight my talents beyond kickball, but this time I could. The final straw in the marriage involved a variety of conflicts, but what stands out in my mind most is a fight over the price of Charmin toilet paper. My heart told me I deserved better. It wasn't about toilet paper or clothes or hairstyles or jobs, it was about knowing that I was good enough to move on. A marriage didn't define success. The transition back to singlehood was difficult, but I survived, opening a door of possibilities as a woman and for my career.

And to this day, I only use one brand of toilet paper.... Charmin!

"Rhonard Park," California

I never saw my ex-husband again. I excelled at picking up the pieces of my life, finishing my graduate program, and securing a job in training and development at a law firm. Ready to take on any challenge, I saw glimmers of my childhood personality return; I was happy.

I liked my job, but this was my first exposure to working with lawyers in a professional space. My graduate degree and experience meant nothing to my colleagues. I was told I was valued but fell quickly into the role of glorified administrator. I was told that the courses I designed were "bad," humiliated for spelling Rohnert Park, California as "Rhonard Park," and felt like I'd never please anyone. The question was back: "Am I good enough to work here?"

It felt like I was back on that kickball field and in the bad marriage at the same time. My heart told me that the best thing I could do in this situation was learn all I could and keep moving. It would be a stop on the journey but not my final destination. I secured a second graduate degree and my beloved doctorate, while even earning a promotion! I had beat the odds, earned credibility with a tough crowd, and my credential. I've been told that many "normal" people would have stopped right here, having earned a great promotion at a great firm, but I wanted more. My heart told me I needed more.

I was very clear that I wanted more responsibilities and opportunities, and that I'd seek them out if they were not made available. While the promotion did come, it came too late. I had been in talks with other firms during the final semester of my doctoral program, interviewed, and thought I found the right fit. When it came time to tell my firm that I was moving on, emotions were mixed. My head boss was not happy and my direct boss said that he didn't think "anything would happen that fast." These reactions caused me to raise the question, "Am I good enough to be moving on?"

Thanksgiving Turkeys and Winter Retreats

Since ending my marriage, I'd wanted to move and was thrilled that my new role came with a free ticket to relocate. I loved moving to Washington, D.C., and the new firm gave me access to direct leadership and the opportunity to really learn how law firms were run. I had face time and the respect of many senior partners. I felt important. At the same time, I had culture shock because it was a much smaller environment than what I was used to. It operated with an "all hands on deck" approach and felt like a small town where everyone knew your business. It was hard to trust people. I was working far beyond the scope of a learning professional and there was a lot I didn't understand—for example, why I was tasked with things involving such a wide range, from attorney terminations to planning Thanksgiving turkey events for the office. I didn't understand why I had to pander to junior staff. I didn't understand

Chapter 2
Great Enough

why planning a firm winter retreat fell on my shoulders though I had no event planning experience.

I again asked myself, "Am I good enough to be wanting more?" mainly because I wasn't happy. The feeling of importance, high salary, and respect from senior partners weren't enough. Back to the kickball field, the bad marriage, and being reprimanded for misspelling a city I had never heard of. Despite that, I felt that gutsy child coming back and knew I needed to admit to myself and others that I could not do it anymore. I felt the presence of my childhood personality because I admitted during my exit interview that this was the dumbest job I had ever had but also the one where I learned the most!

Around the World in Six Years

My experience and connections allowed me to score a global role and I again relocated, this time to New York City. When sharing the news of my new role and upcoming move with friends, I was told by a particularly critical and outspoken one, "I don't see you in New York." Back came the self-doubt, "Am I good enough to be given this opportunity and to live in New York?"

In many ways, the six years that followed were the best of my life thus far. The new job was everything I had hoped for—I got to focus only on my area of expertise and travel around the world for firm development activities. But these opportunities came with a fresh set of critical eyes and workplace bullies. People who had no experience in my field weighed in, making it hard to meet deliverables. While I was happy in theory, I began losing myself yet again. Lost in travel, lost in judgment, lost in bullying, and lost in my own head.

The world took a dark turn in 2020. Not only was I restricted to a seven-hundred-fifty-square-foot apartment, but everyone had opinions about everything. I had so many fears, from death to losing my livelihood to never seeing my loved ones again. I lost friends, some over conflicts with the pandemic and some because their true colors (i.e., jealousy and competition) surfaced.

Thanks to the power of vaccines, I returned to my old life, but it felt different. The anxiety was still there...so bad that I remember being in a hotel bathroom over the July 4th weekend, thinking I was having a heart attack. I was relieved when it turned out to be a panic attack, but I couldn't figure out why this had happened. When I learned that I had some health issues, I sensed there was more to it than that. Maybe it was my heart's way of telling me to make some permanent changes.

Team Sabrina

I needed help. I am close to my family but didn't share the details of this struggle because it felt too personal. As a woman, it's hard to admit when you are hurting. But I took the necessary steps to commit to a wellness journey, conquering my fear of doctors and following the advice I was given. I formulated a team of healers, including an amazing female doctor, two wonderful chiropractors, and a yoga therapist, and fondly nicknamed them "Team Sabrina." Team Sabrina inspired me to slow down, take time off and travel for me, and also to begin to accept myself as an intelligent, beautiful, and powerful woman. My life became less about work and more about me. More about finding the balance between the two forces and learning to forgive myself for not being perfect. I rewarded myself with two Hawaiian vacations and did some major reflection on what I would and would not tolerate.

I learned that I tolerated too much from others; I had also made a lot of mistakes, the largest of which was constantly questioning myself. I forgave myself when I realized that I had "missed" some of my greatest moments in life because I expected too much from myself. I allowed myself to be taken advantage of because I did not know how to set boundaries.

I credit Team Sabrina, and myself, for helping me have these realizations. When it came time for me to make another career-

Chapter 2
Great Enough

altering decision, I decided to accept the new role because I never once asked myself, "Am I good enough for this opportunity?" I knew I was!

Hawaiian Love Affair

I rarely think about the kickball days, bad marriage, health issues, childhood and workplace bullying, and dark career moments with regret. They are true heart whispers, moments that defined me and allowed me to become an amazing, thriving woman. I can say that I am back to my childhood personality—now I just need to come up with forty-something versions of running around in my underwear and spraying my aunts with the Fun Fountain!

I was fortunate enough to take a six-week leave before stepping into my current role. I spent most of it in my new favorite place, Hawaii. About to celebrate another trip around the sun, I asked the question one final time while watching a fabulous sunset over the island of Kauai—"Am I good enough?" This time I answered myself by saying, "You are not good enough, and you are *GREAT* enough."

ABOUT THE AUTHOR: Dr. Sabrina Franconeri is a learning and development professional with a passion for inspiring people through educational journeys. Dr. Franconeri has spent more than twenty years teaching the importance of understanding communication styles. Born in Ft. Lauderdale, Florida, Dr. Franconeri spent much of her life in Pittsburgh, Pennsylvania, earning her Doctor of Science in Communications at Robert Morris University. She has lived in Washington, D.C. and currently lives and works in the New York City area. Dr. Franconeri loves to travel and considers Hawaii her home away from home. She attributes her love of learning to her parents.

Dr. Sabrina Franconeri
sabrina2079@gmail.com

CHAPTER 3

Your Heart Will Lead You Home

How I Left the Dark Room and Rebuilt My Life

Lin Moctezuma

Did you ever wake up one day and not know who you were anymore? There are things that have happened in my life that have shaken me to the very core. I felt the same horrible feelings all the time. Anxiety, depression, and hopelessness ran my life.

I come from a very broken family, with mental, physical, verbal, and sexual abuse that unfortunately was passed down through generations, including my own.

I was eighteen years old when I got married the first time and had my first child at nineteen. By the time my son was five, I had purchased my first home because I wanted to provide a better life for him, away from the troubled neighborhood we were living in. Shortly after purchasing the house, I was laid off from my job due to budget cuts. My first thought was, *How was I going to pay that mortgage?* I remember driving home that day feeling hopeless like my world was over. Little did I know the upheaval was just beginning.

Not long after losing my job, I filed for divorce after finding out that my husband was having an affair. Every piece of my life seemed to be falling apart, and my stress and anxiety kept growing. How was I going to make it as a single mom? I was in what's called the "Crazy 8," bouncing back and forth between depression and anger, sadness and worry. I tried hard to keep it all together for the sake of my son, but there were times when my anger took the best of me. I had my hands full trying to keep up with the bills, the mortgage payment, and making sure we had food on the table. Many times, I had to decide *between* paying the bills and putting food on the table.

No one knew my struggles because I never wanted to let people in. I not only hid behind a fake smile, I was also very good at internalizing my emotions and stress to the point of becoming very physically ill. Most days, I didn't feel like waking up and told myself I was just tired and felt like "sleeping in." The truth was, I was in a very dark place. This is the place where you feel helpless. Where days blend into each other and time has no value. It's a place where you don't care too much about anything. It's a period in your life where the world could be hurting and you don't seem to care. You feel like you're numb to pain. Darkness feels like you are trapped in your head and having a never-ending conversation with yourself that you can't take a break from. The gist of that conversation is that you are the victim.

After years of struggling as a single mom, I met my second husband; we married a year later. Things were going great; we were happy. Then, two years into the marriage, I learned I was pregnant, never imagining that this would set our relationship on a completely different path. Shortly after the baby came, we both started to see red flags. We weren't communicating, and when we did, it was to argue; frustration, resentment, deception, and lack of trust took over our once "perfect" marriage.

We started to realize that we had both come to the relationship

Chapter 3
Your Heart Will Lead You Home

with "baggage." We were not as ready as we thought we were. We were being triggered by situations, yet we didn't even know they were triggers. We were seeing these triggers as issues in our marriage. I became very distant from my husband; I no longer felt happy, the arguments and disappointments became bigger, and I found myself in a very dark place yet again. I was hurt, sad, depressed; I felt betrayed and lied to, and I feared the worst.

I would lock myself in the room for days at a time and not talk to him or anyone else. I cried all the time, and every day that I was locked in that room, these thoughts ran on a loop: "How do I end this?"; "Why am I like this?"; "Why do I react the way I do?"; "Why do things bother me so much?"; "Why was I brought on this earth to just suffer?" It was always a "Why? Why? Why?"

I had deep-rooted scars as a result of emotional and psychological trauma that had left me struggling with upsetting emotions, memories, and anxiety. It also made me feel numb, disconnected, and unable to trust other people. Every hour of the day, I felt like vomiting because of the stress. I even played with the idea of just ending it all, of taking my own life, but there was something inside of me that kept saying I had to fight. That voice in my head would remind me that as strong as I was, I also had to remember that I was vulnerable. Once again, no one knew of the battle raging in my heart, mind, and ego.

I knew I was at a crossroads, that the decision I was about to make would impact the rest of my life. I had been holding onto the idea that my marriage was perfect. I also thought that a good marriage was not vulnerable to insecurities and triggers. When the problems got bigger, I saw my husband as a coward because he never took responsibility for his actions. He deflected in every conversation. As far as I was concerned, this marriage had reached its demise.

When I filed for divorce, we were barely speaking to each other.

The marshal served him the papers while he was in the living room, and I was crying in the bedroom. After I filed for divorce the dark nights in a room by myself continued as I blamed my past, I blamed my husband, I blamed my family. I was the victim of another failed marriage. My hopes and dreams were shattered, and I thought my life was over. The thoughts of suicide continued to flood my head. When things go haywire, we tend to cling to our irrational thoughts like a life-preserver when what we really need to hold onto is our inner calm.

I really believed that I could just think my way out of the hopelessness box I had placed myself in. I obsessed over my problems, trying to make sense out of every conversation, but it never made sense. Nothing was ever good enough; nothing was ever good at all. And there seemed nothing I could do about it but obsess even more.

Then I had a light bulb moment: I realized that all these thoughts were keeping me from thinking about the real problem. The real reason I was uncomfortable and stuck in this thought loop was because of my own insecurities and deeply-rooted self-worth issues. The obsessive thoughts kept me looking past the fact that all this started and ended with me. Often, when you think defeating and self-limiting thoughts all day, you start to believe they are true.

How did I learn this? First, I was doing a lot of journaling, which helped me to recognize the patterns in my thoughts. Second, a friend handed me a Tony Robbins book. Immediately, I was hooked; I was hungry for more knowledge. I wanted to keep reading and learning about his strategy, his tools. Reading this book changed my life. I saw that everything I was going through—every struggle, pain, and hardship—was actually a gift. It was a gift because in the struggle, I questioned the purpose of my life. It is a gift because it forced me to dig deeper within myself. I was learning to get out of my head

Chapter 3
Your Heart Will Lead You Home

and listen to my heart.

This was the beginning of my path to healing. I have since learned that I was also to blame for the demise of the marriage. I had a lot of faults; I was empty inside. I had no love for myself, no self-worth. I learned that I needed to get help and get to the root of my problems if I ever want to have a successful relationship with anyone. I needed to take care of myself and, as Tony Robbins said, "change the narrative of my story and my belief system." I began extensive therapy to work on myself; I started to learn a lot about myself; I continued to journal and read self-help books. In addressing my inner thoughts and emotions, I finally started to confront some of the beliefs that had kept me stuck. I was learning the ability to look within myself because I was curious about my fundamental purpose in life.

After I filed for divorce my ex-husband also began his own healing journey, including therapy. Over the next three years, we both did a lot of self-reflecting and personal growth work that led to greater self-awareness. It was about slowing down to listen to our thoughts, emotions, and body signals. I learned to accept and love myself and I started to feel the inner peace and calm inside.

We all have faced some sort of struggle or hardship in life. We have all hurt, physically or emotionally, and may still be in pain now. Oftentimes, we feel betrayed by life itself; we feel it is unfair and question why we have to go through these struggles. What we don't realize is that these struggles—be it an illness, a relationship breakdown, or financial ruin—are gifts.

The courage it took for me to leave behind what was not for me anymore was the same courage that helped me find what I wanted to do with my life. What I focused on became my reality. I enrolled in Robbins/Madanes Core 100 program and took part in Tony's Unshakable Challenge for the first time. Let me tell you, it was a real eye-opener. It couldn't have come at a better time.

As a result of the inner work we had been doing, my husband and I were able to rebuild our marriage. This time, we came together with clear heads and a new perspective on life, marriage, and communication. We each took ownership, responsibility, and action to change what needed to be changed to get our relationship back on track and thriving again.

I am living proof that if you follow your heart and never give up, you will always find your happily ever after. I've learned that with a can-do attitude I can make it all work. I wish I knew back then what I know now, but I also know that everything happens for a reason. All my struggles, traumas, and lessons all happened *for* me, not *to* me, but to change me for the better. I had to go through the lessons in order to be where I am today. I have recognized that love is a verb, an action and that I must live that love to feel it every day. I know now that love is primary…life may bring annoyances and grievances, but the love must come first. Communication is also critical. No matter how much you love someone and how in sync you are, neither of you are mind-readers. You must speak your thoughts, your fears, and your joys because all of it matters and is more important than you know. If you start from a place of love and acceptance for yourself, it greatly affects the way you think about important things in your life. My husband and I have an incredible relationship and we continue to put in the work to maintain it—every day.

I want you to find true happiness and peace within your soul. Remember to love yourself. Embrace happiness. Pursue your dreams. You are in control of your own future and the people you choose to share your life with.

Chapter 3
Your Heart Will Lead You Home

ABOUT THE AUTHOR: When people experience trauma or severe life stressors, it's common for their lives to unravel. Lin Moctezuma is a Certified Life Coach; her first book is Manage Your Stress ~ Master Your Life. Her passion is bringing healing to people who have been through traumatic and stressful experiences by teaching them the tools they need to handle stress. Prior to her writing career, Lin graduated from the Robbins-Madanes Training/RMT Center Core 100 program. Lin's personal journey has included many challenges and victories; it also led her to discover her passion for helping others. She is known for her kind-hearted, nurturing, and compassionate coaching style.

Lin Moctezuma
Lin the Life Coach
linlifecoach.com
linlifecoach@gmail.com
860-785-5917

CHAPTER 4

Just Say YES!

Carrie Clark

It was a typical Monday morning. I slogged my way to the bathroom and looked in the mirror, not recognizing the thirty-nine-year-old woman staring back at me. She had large bags under her eyes and they were swollen from crying. Her mouth was in a permanent frown and her gaze was hollow. Who was she?

There I was, a mother of two young boys who needed my constant attention and a wife trying to keep up with my marriage and household demands—all while working a full-time job. I was miserable. Each day had the sweet parts of being a mother who absolutely loved her kids, but mostly each day was just sad. Frustration, anger, and cheerlessness were weaved into the daily routine, weighing me down and robbing me of happiness.

It was not always this way. *I* was not always this way. I felt like I was on autopilot, trying not to feel much at all. It seemed so much easier to just let life pass me by.

And it wasn't just my home life. Work was mind-numbing. I had gone from a fast-paced career producing events in New York City to a dull desk job I could do in my sleep. I took this position because I was overwhelmed with trying to balance my crazy work hours with motherhood. I wanted to think I could do it all, but each day seemed to present me with evidence to the contrary. Finally, and upon the advice of my husband and parents, I took that darn desk job. I wanted out as quickly as I got in. There was no challenge, no excitement. There was also no potential financial growth—I had capped out on that a few short years before. I missed "the climb" and felt handcuffed to a job I was great at but did not love.

By this point, exhaustion, depression, defeat, and sadness had been my sidekicks for five years. My marriage, when it was at its best, was like walking a tightrope. At any moment I could fall into full-on despair. I could not breathe.

One night, when I actually had a moment to myself, I was lying in bed scrolling through social media on my iPad when I came across an ad for a six-week self-help program. I wanted to pass by it—who needs self-help, right?—but something quiet and persistent made me stop for a closer look. The next thing I knew I had my credit card in hand to order this "life uplevel" program. I had no idea how it would work, if at all, yet I plunged forward in quiet hopeful faith.

When the uplevel program finally arrived, I opened the package to find a huge binder of worksheets and CDs (this was back when we actually had something to play CDs on). Each night, I followed the steps one page at a time. It was a beautiful recipe for gradual transformation that included faith, hope, forgiveness, positive self-talk, healing, and most of all, gratitude. Feeling the shift, I remember feeling lighter with that glimmer of hope growing. Time had in store for me a greater love and outlook. Slowly the fog began to lift and I started doing small things for myself like yoga and visiting with friends.

It was around this time that a guest speaker came to my job to present on energy leadership. I loved her content and connection. More than that, I got a sense that this was what I was meant to do. I was meant to speak and tell others how to be fully YOU in work and in life. Again, I heard that quiet, gentle but persistent voice

Chapter 4
Just Say YES!

nudging me, saying "You can do this. You can get up in front of people and speak. You are meant to do this, just like her."

In high school and college, I got into theater, an experience that broke me out of my shell and gave me a voice of confidence. I gained an outward attitude of self-love and advocacy. Unfortunately, that had all been lost somewhere between partying in my early twenties to adulting in all things—career, marriage, and kids.

That evening, on a dime, I created space to research how that speaker got to where she was in her business and her career. I discovered she was a professional certified coach. At the time I didn't even know what coaching was, but I felt a glimmer of excitement start to grow inside my heart. A part of me had no idea where I was going with this, and the other part of me said, "Go, go, go!" Over the next week I did a lot of research on coaching certifications, including interviewing others who had gone through the process, and finally decided on a robust coaching program that was both in person and online over a period of three months.

I was apprehensive and excited at the same time. However, two things were against me. The first was the ongoing turmoil in my personal life, though my outlook was better than before. Thing two was the price tag: a hefty ten thousand dollars. How in the world would I justify doing this? It was at that moment that I remembered the money I had been secretly storing away for that maybe, one day, if-and-when divorce.

Ultimately, I couldn't deny the pull. I signed up for the program and announced it to my family. As you can imagine, my family—especially my husband—were in shock. Whether they liked it or not, I was pushing through my fear and just going for it. The world had conspired to welcome me back to the land of the living and inspired me to love myself again.

I dove headfirst into a huge period of growth and understanding of myself. In learning how to coach others, I slowly learned even more about how to heal myself. I discovered all the things I was doing that had held me back for so long. I took a hard look at my sometimes dark, destructive thoughts and found the tools to turn them around to paint a better life outlook for myself and my well-being.

Even as I applied all I was learning to myself, there was a great deal of resistance. In the beginning, I resisted the energy leadership piece and found it a bit hokey, a little too over-the-top and, shall I say, "too happy." I also struggled with the notion of coaching others when I could barely keep myself afloat. Looking back, that inner work was like peeling away layers of a rotten onion to reveal that the outer layers were not rotten at all, but merely ineffective self-protection. And underneath those layers, I found my truth. Heart expansion. Growth. Attainable happiness?

Before I knew it, I was halfway through the course. I had already met some wonderful like-minded classmates face-to-face in the first of three long-weekend classes. Now I was anticipating the next one. I asked out loud and from my heart for a new friend to enter my life through coaching. I wanted someone who lived close by and with whom I could share in this coaching work. Enter Jenny—wildly warm and intense, deep and beautiful, creative and inspiring. She had not been present at the earlier in-person weekend, yet there she was at the second. That heartfelt prayer to meet a friend with whom I could share this coaching gift had just been manifested. I do not know any other way to describe it.

Jenny also lived very close to me—thanks, again, Universe!—and we started meeting for lunch on occasion. We wanted to create a way to teach others the techniques we'd learned, not just through one-on-one coaching but in a bigger way. During one of those conversations, the spark came: we would create a Meetup group called "Say Yes To You." Each month we met for talks, teachings, and adventures. We dove into subjects like rewriting your story, reducing stress, energy leadership, and healing, among many others.

Chapter 4
Just Say YES!

The teaching part energized me and lit me up in ways I had not felt in a very long time. Even more than that, it gave me the opportunity to get used to speaking in front of people. It made me let go of the fear of trying out new things. It helped me learn, grow, and push through my limits of being scared to speak up. Each day, I started to play a little bit bigger than I had before.

It was around this time that a leader and friend at work caught wind that I was creating and presenting on subjects like stress reduction and goal-setting. She invited me to present at work, and before I knew it I was embarking on a wild journey, speaking about stress reduction at our offices throughout the Northeast. During these presentations we had fun with vision boards, stress management, and creating space for oneself. I learned so much from others on career struggles and challenges that I was inspired to create a workshop on Work-Life Harmony which I presented in the Say Yes To You group and in various cities.

One evening, while scrolling through social media, I came across a call for speakers for the Global Business Travel Association. Being in the events industry, I had heard of this reputable association before. Feeling that now-familiar pull, I applied, happily knowing that it was a complete long shot. I felt safe in the perceived knowledge that they would never pick me. I was mistaken.

Months later, I received a note that I'd been selected to be a speaker for their annual convention in Chicago. This was a big deal. Huge. I was elated. Fear kicked in double-time too, but this time I knew better and did not listen to all the things that could possibly get in the way. I replied with a resounding YES, as in, "I will be there. I will do this thing."

To this point I had gone from the classroom to speaking at work, our Meetup group, and in many libraries. This, however, was a true upleveling experience, with a microphone, audiovisual, and a built-in audience. Needless to say, it was both thrilling and terrifying, and

I would not have traded it for anything. Deep breaths. This time I was not the person sitting in the audience wondering what it would be like to be the speaker. I WAS the speaker!

During this trip I got to meet other speakers who inspired me. I forged friendships and connections, and it paved the way for other wonderful opportunities for coaching and experiences leading talks. Amazing!

Even more amazing is that I modeled what I taught. I came to love consistent meditation, practicing gratitude, forgiveness, self-reflection, and developing my spiritual journey. I expanded my joy. My life and the power of saying yes to myself expanded inward and outward with boundless possibilities.

As a result of this transformation, my marriage grew to be loving and hopeful again. After all, I was fifty percent of the equation, and I had learned so much about being a loving partner and friend. I learned to love and to let things be. Peace and hope were inspired by beautiful moments in our relationship. As I got stronger, so did we.

As for my career, I received a prestigious award in the company I was working for. My personal glow and desire to help others were catching on. Even the ringtone on my phone—"This Girl is on Fire"—provided constant affirmation of this path of my heart song. My empowered journey had only just begun.

Eventually, I went for and received one of my dream jobs leading a team in the company I so loved. When I lost that job during the pandemic, I greeted it, not as a catastrophe, but yet another beautiful chapter in my story. This continues to be a journey of turning inspired thoughts into inspired action on a dime, building positive momentum for the blessings that lay ahead. As the heart whispers, the truth will be revealed in grace and gratitude.

Chapter 4
Just Say YES!

ABOUT THE AUTHOR: Carrie Clark is a talented speaker, author, and Energy Leadership coach who helps people tap into their intuition and uplevel their personal and professional lives. Carrie's unique techniques allow individuals to take purposeful action steps to say YES to themselves. With a passion for empowering others, Carrie has spoken on stages to associations and organizations on the topics of self-mastery, confidence, and work life harmony. Carrie's engaging work helps serve clients and audiences to optimize their careers and lives holistically by focusing on personal core values, positive mindset shifts, intention setting, and boundary optimization to create their best lives.

Carrie Clark, ACC SHRM-CP, ELI MP
Carrie Clark Coaching LLC
sayyes2you.com ~ carrie@sayyes2you.com
LinkedIn: linkedin.com/in/carrie-clark-cpc
Instagram: @carrieclarkcpc

CHAPTER 5

Leading with a Courageous Heart
Divinely Aligned Messages in Action

Dr. Lara May

Midway through a graveyard shift in the fall of 2014, I found myself lying on the cold floor of the pharmacy. All the lights were off, and I was trying to will the pain in my head to fade and the waves of nausea to stop—an exercise as futile as trying to stop the waves of the ocean. At this time of night there was no one to call in to help me, and even if there was, I probably couldn't have made the seventy-mile drive home. Why, I wondered for the hundredth time, did I keep choosing my work over my health? Why did I keep pushing myself into positions that, if I was being honest with myself, weren't even fulfilling? They were killing me, instigating and inflaming my chronic migraines, fueling my depressive eating and drinking, and sending my IBS to new extremes. I wasn't supposed to be this sick—nobody should be—and certainly not at thirty-four! On the outside, I looked like a healthy, active person. I was an avid, year-round backcountry athlete in the Sierra Nevada Mountains, and had a successful career as a clinical pharmacist in large and small hospitals across Northern California. I also had a wonderful relationship with the man I loved. Sure, I carried a little extra weight, but who doesn't these days?

A year and a half earlier, I had left my dream job in a busy Sacramento emergency room to be closer to, and more consistently present with, my partner of three years. I had spent two of those years alternating weeks between Sacramento and Tahoe, where we lived, and it was starting to take its toll on the relationship. I had a choice to make—keep the job I loved, had trained and studied so hard for and put in years of work to get, or a relationship that was full of love, adventure, and so much potential. In the end, I listened to my heart and took a local position in Tahoe.

Little did I know that this decision would change the trajectory of my life. While the relationship flourished, my satisfaction with my career took a nosedive. I tried to convince myself that it was "just a job" and that I could focus on all the other amazing aspects of my life. I could ignore all the ways my soul was crying out for connection. It was during this time that I started eating and drinking to soothe and suppress my emotions.

I eventually got another job that allowed me to work seven days on, seven off—a great schedule for traveling and other things I enjoyed. There were two catches, however: the job was seventy miles from home and it required me to work the graveyard shift. But hey, sleep is overrated, right? It was the time not spent at work that was really important. At least that what's I told myself, until the migraines got so bad I couldn't feel my hands, and so frequent that at least one or two days of my work week were spent lying on that floor, in physical and emotional agony.

It was during this dark night of the soul that I started searching for answers outside of allopathic medicine. All the meds that were supposed to prevent and stop my myriad of health problems hadn't done that at all. In fact, everything seemed to be progressing forward at an unnerving rate.

My search led me to functional medicine and reiki, both of which resonated deeply with my soul. It didn't take long to realize that I had found not only a path to healing but my life path as a teacher and practitioner.

Chapter 5
Leading with a Courageous Heart

Opening my mind, heart, body, and Soul to the practice of Usui and Angelic reiki opened a connection with my higher self, and to the Divine, which I had shut off long ago. I was raised in the Southern Baptist church, and while this community cultivated my love and expression of music, there was also an environment of judgment and hypocrisy that I witnessed and experienced. As a result, I turned away from Divine guidance and, at the wise old age of eighteen, declared myself an atheist. I put my faith in science and the empiric, and even when I studied religion and philosophy in college it was from an analytical, historical perspective. My life was dedicated to science, the function of the human body, the operation of medications in and on the body, and healing through contemporary technology. That which could be seen, studied, replicated, and published was valid; anything heart-based or spiritual was not even considered.

But at the lowest of my low—lost, sick, and disillusioned with Western medicine and the way it treats healthcare workers, the paradigm I'd lived by began to crumble. Through my self-reiki practice, I was feeling shifts, seeing changes, releasing old, trapped emotions, and opening up to the possibilities of miraculous healing. The more consistent I was in this practice, the more resources and people in alignment with this shift showed up. My mind and body were starting to come back into connection and synchronization. I reconnected with my breath through yoga and meditation, realizing what a powerful tool of change we all have naturally within us.

Yoga was a godsend, a means of merging movement and meditation to further support the movement of energy through my body. Parallel with this unfolding were visits to my first functional medicine practitioner, who took the time to test my body systems on a deeper level than any other physicians even knew was available. I learned about the root causes of inflammation and started to connect our root biological functions with the energetic laws of the universe. My fascination with merging the physical healing journey with the energetic healing journey was born.

I started to have a deep understanding of the true connection between our minds, bodies, and souls. It is no accident, and it cannot be escaped. I saw that the more I shut down certain parts of my body and emotions, the more upheaval materialized in my life. I felt the truth of the saying, "We are spiritual beings having a human experience," not the other way around. Humans are an integral piece of the universal flow, of the cosmic field of infinite potential, the quantum. To live a fulfilled life of love, happiness, and connection, we must be awake, aware, aligned, and deliberate participants in our actions and choices.

What does alignment mean? What does it look like? For me, it entails a daily intentional meditation of connecting with Source and opening my energetic centers to receive from and commune with angels, ascended masters, and other aspects of the Divine Realms. By doing this, I align my heart with my higher self and Divine vibration, which allows me to receive clear guidance and take inspired action. It is a specific vibrational existence that is deliberately chosen.

This practice became imperative to my survival while working in acute care hospitals during the height of the COVID pandemic. I was not expecting the changes I saw in our healthcare system. Physicians' choices to treat their patients as they saw fit were taken away and replaced with a protocolized system they dare not veer from. The workplace became hostile, distrusting, judgmental, and retaliatory in many departments and on many levels. Many days, the constant reminders to myself that I was there to serve the patients, the most vulnerable, was the only thing that kept me coming back.

It's much easier to be a follower, to go through life without questioning authority, but that has never been my nature. I am a truth-seeker and an advocate for the best possible strategies and outcomes for my patients and myself. Back when I was first

Chapter 5
Leading with a Courageous Heart

learning reiki, I began to say an invocation of the Angelic Realm for protection and healing of myself, the hospital, my patients, and all the practitioners every night before I even walked in the door.

During COVID this invocation became all the more imperative. Again, doctors were being told they could only make practice decisions within a very narrow scope of options. They were threatened with the loss of their jobs if they stepped outside that scope—as were the pharmacists. In the past, guidelines had been just that—guidelines. Now, they were commandments to be followed without question. Again, I saw the judgment of my colleagues against those they disagreed with. We had all taken oaths, to "do no harm" and treat everyone the same and with equal respect, but fear and uncertainty of COVID put on display the default unconscious behavior of humanity, and it wasn't pretty.

This time, instead of building walls around myself, I mustered the courage to lead with my heart. I spoke up to challenge practices and vaccine mandates and support colleagues through the process of applying for exemptions and appeals. I spoke up for other treatment options that were evidence-based but not bought and paid for by big pharma. And finally, after being with the same healthcare company for ten years, I decided to explore other options. I knew my value, and I knew my passion and commitment to healing could be seen, recognized, and appreciated at many other places across the country. I was tired of being told no over and over and seeing people die needlessly. I was determined to step into my courage, lead with conviction, and advocate for real healing, rather than band-aid medicine.

For the first time, I started to consider forming my own full-time health coaching practice—one in which I could incorporate the energetic healing of angelic reiki with the powerful root cause approach of functional medicine. A practice where I could practice with integrity and autonomy and actually see my patients get well.

Today I am still a part-time clinical pharmacist practicing in acute care hospitals, but I also have that private practice I dreamed of where true healing takes place. Through the ups and downs, the trials and tribulations, I found my voice, found my passion and conviction, and my courage to lead by example. It is my mission to change how we view "healthcare." Humans are powerful creators and that includes health and wellness, and that's what I empower and teach to my clients.

ABOUT THE AUTHOR: Dr. Lara May is an Advanced Practice Clinical Pharmacist, Functional Medicine Health Coach, and Master Attuned Intuitive Healer and Teacher who specializes in getting to the root cause of disease via functional medicine and energy medicine. After working in emergency rooms and adult acute care for over a decade, she transitioned into integrative health. Due to her struggle with her own health, Lara started studying and practicing Usui & Angelic reiki in 2014, then functional medicine health coaching in 2017. Lara's passion and mission is to empower patients to take an active role in their well-being, so they can create their health on their terms.

Dr. Lara May, PharmD, BCPS, APh, CFMP
Light Body Healing & Consulting, LLC
drlaramay.com
laramay@drlaramy.com
530-212-0024

CHAPTER 6

Nurturing Synergy Through the Union of Spirit and Science

Sharon Montes, M.D.

I start and end this chapter with gratitude for all my teachers, who have generously shared their wisdom.

Our hearts speak to us in whispers. Our most profound wisdom and guidance come, not from our thinking minds, but from our hearts. Our heart doesn't shout, nag, or shrilly demand our attention. Nurturing our capacity to align and connect with heart whispers helps us live with vibrant health, make better decisions, communicate more effectively, and live with greater passion and purpose. Our heart whispers give us life *WOWS*.

In a world that often values achievement and productivity over well-being and fulfillment, it is easy to lose touch with our inner guidance and prioritize external expectations over our own needs and desires. Women often juggle multiple life roles—professional, partner, homemaker, caregiver, friend, daughter, mother, and more. Balancing these roles can be challenging, and we often end up neglecting our needs in the process. This is the victory of head chatter over heart whispers.

As a holistic physician and a woman who has been through this journey, I want to share how I designed a life I love by listening to my innate wisdom and nurturing myself—and how you can too.

Synergy 1 + 1 = 3 My Personal Connection With ALL

I am the child of an artist mother and a scientist father. Although vastly different in personality and communication styles, my parents were united in their love of nature and commitment to parenting. Mom processed sensory information through light and color. She created beauty in the forms of paintings, pottery, sewing, crocheting, and teaching art to others. In contrast, Dad processed and expressed himself through words and numbers, creating beauty in the form of writing, research, and educating others about land use and conservation. I developed a respect for both. I grew up on a small farm where I learned to clean barns, create garden soil, care for aggressive geese in freezing weather, and grow, harvest, and preserve food. My farmer and social worker ancestors contributed to my respect for life and understanding that health happens from the ground up and in community.

In 1971, as an eleven-year-old walking alone along a dirt road in the woods on the upper peninsula of Michigan, I had a life-changing experience. I sensed myself as a light, and felt a deep, unified light-filled connection with all that was around me. I was in an expanded sense of NOW. That encounter with what could be called "cosmic consciousness," that sense of connection with all life, continues to influence me. Today I have a variety of words to point to that awareness and experience—Source, Creator, God, or even Agape. Words describe but don't duplicate that sense of oneness, and I respect the words others use to describe what unifies us all.

My family started exploring meditation and Eastern religious traditions in 1975, practicing yoga in our living room on Sunday mornings and taking a class for each of us to receive a "mantra." We learned a practice of meditation that involved sitting still with eyes closed and mentally repeating a single-syllable seed sound.

In high school, one of my most influential classes was Comparative Religions. We first studied familiar Western religions, followed by

Chapter 6
Nurturing Synergy Through the Union of Spirit and Science

the Eastern religions of Hinduism, Buddhism, and Confucianism. I was struck by the fact that, if there is only one God or single unifying force, humans have, through religion, created many systems and paths to connect with that God. In college I took as many comparative religion classes as I did biology classes. I remained curious about religious systems, yet committed to my individual alignment and connection with what I called spirituality; for me, it was beyond words, and sometimes other people's structures interfered with my experience.

In 1995, I had some biofeedback done while I meditated. The measurements of my skin, muscles, and heart rate showed I had spent twenty years meditating as a practice of dissociating rather than improving my health. This information was both surprising and extremely valuable, as it solidified the value of combining the wisdom of science and spirit. It also changed my meditation practices. I still used words, mantras, and affirmations as a banana for my monkey mind but included more use of movement, breath, and neurofeedback (even before Joe Dispenza :o) I learned the value of carrying a "meditative" state into my waking life—eyes and heart open.

Synergy 1 + 1 = 3: My Professional Integration of East and West

My career choice as a holistic physician was an attempt to reconcile and integrate both of my parents' influences, a connection with life, and a commitment to serve others and evolve spiritually. Eventually, it led to integrating Eastern and Western health systems into my work. This has required a life-long commitment to learning and expressing both art and science with the wisdom experienced in studying both science and spirituality.

At the end of my family medicine residency in a regional trauma center, I registered for a community class in acupressure. I was delighted to learn about this Eastern health system based on energy flow, and correspondences between seasons, senses, emotions, and organs, with no artificial barriers between mind and body. I spent ten years practicing acupuncture and teaching it to other physicians. Helping create conditions for people to heal themselves by restoring balance—removing toxins and nourishing the good stuff—applies to both Eastern and Western healing approaches.

I was blessed to spend sixteen years teaching in medical schools, honoring, and respecting pharmaceuticals and technology coupled with the capacity to keep people alive and help them heal from severe physical trauma. I also taught about "alternative" medicine that has now grown to be called Integrative Medicine. I helped plant the seeds for medical and nursing students and community members, about other healing traditions, herbal medicine, energy medicine, acupuncture, and mindfulness.

My current integration of the wisdom of science and spirit includes using technology in my coaching programs. The Positive Intelligence App, for example, beautifully combines the power of small, daily change with easy access to the mind-body practices I have spent fifty years learning and teaching. By "gamifying" mental fitness, this app allows people to "upgrade" their personal operating system by building and developing their own Sage powers.

The Power of Three

As humans, we have been blessed with not one brain, but three. My goal is to integrate all of them to harmonize, align, and respect the wisdom from each.

The Head brain is about thinking and reasoning; it observes the world. It is divided into right and left hemispheres and fueled by chemicals—neurotransmitters and peptides that influence consciousness.

The Heart, or emotional, brain is the seat of our emotional intelligence, allowing us to resonate with others, and is based on electromagnetic fields. The heart's electromagnetic field is one hundred times greater than that of our head and brain, and generates

Chapter 6
Nurturing Synergy Through the Union of Spirit and Science

an electrical wave of sixty times greater amplitude than that created by our thinking brains; it is five thousand times greater than the field created by our thinking brains. I generally follow the lead of my Heart-brain. Using this inner GPS, I "sense" the path offering the most light, knowing the logic for that decision will generally follow.

And, last but not least, we have the Gut, or knowing, brain, which is the seat of our sensing or instinctual abilities. There is a greater number of bacteria in the gut than we have cells in the body, and the presence or lack of balance there plays a critical role in regulating the chemicals that influence our thoughts and emotions.

The vagus nerve, which is the longest cranial nerve in the body, connects the three brains; thus, it is an important path for amplifying our heart whispers and being able to use them as a GPS signal in our daily life.

Learning to pay attention to heart whispers increases our ability to connect with everything in positive ways. The body speaks with energy, not words. The Universe also communicates with energy. Cultivating coherent heart energy impacts both our personal health and the health of others around us.

Daily Intention and the World Beyond Mind Chatter

Our nervous system exists to help us survive and we are wired to receive information from the world around us (e.g., other people's nervous systems, plants, animals, rocks.) It is said that it gathers about eleven million bits of information per second, while our conscious mind processes only about fifty bits per second. Most of our "knowing" is below the conscious level and we are constantly seeking to maintain some sort of balance. We can soothe our nervous systems alone, known as self-regulating, or with others, known as co-regulating. We can also calm our nervous systems in healthy or unhealthy ways. As a highly sensitive introvert who has spent thousands of hours in trauma environments, I've had plenty of experience learning to practice healthy self-regulation. Over the last five years, I have increased my focus on creating healthy co-regulation. As I navigate caring for my elderly parents, I am clear that I am not just asking for help from others; rather, I am being supported by "brains" that expand the capacity of my own nervous system. Engaging others' hearts, hands, and heads in creating a healthy neuro-network for my homestead is especially important as my mom and dad are losing their mental and physical capacities. "Healthy co-regulation" is creating greater ease and grace for our team as we all travel this life journey with my parents.

In Taoism, the goal is to live in proper relationships with ALL—Self, Source, Others, and Nature. In my everyday life, I hold this intention. It is a dynamic flow that changes daily and from season to season.

Below is a list of some things I find helpful in cultivating right relationships and my capacity to live into and from this space of heart whispers. Deliberately schedule a time to do and be in space that allows you to quiet the head chatter, experience and express life beyond words, and consciously cultivate your connection with Source.

1. Connect with Conscious Breathing. For thousands of years, people have been using conscious breath to create greater peace in their body-mind. Different patterns and rates of breathing create different chemical and nervous system patterns. My favorite pattern is called the Physiologic Sigh, the breath that infants use to calm themselves. Inhale through your nose until your lungs are mostly full, then pause briefly and top it off with another inhale. Now, slowly, slowly, slowly exhale out through your mouth. Repeat this two to three times.

2. Connect with Nature. Nature has a way of helping you feel connected to something greater than yourself. Walk in the park, hike in the mountains, spend time in your garden, or simply sit outside listening to the birds and the

Chapter 6
Nurturing Synergy Through the Union of Spirit and Science

trees rustling. Spending time in nature can powerfully cultivate a sense of connection with Source; it can quiet the mind, allowing you to access your inner wisdom.

3. Connect with Music, Art, Math. All of these experiences are expression beyond words. Create your own or appreciate another's creation.

4. Connect with Movement. This can be dancing, sports, tai chi, and yoga, et cetera, alone or in unison with others.

5. Connect with Inspiration. Connect with others who are visionary, inspired, and courageous. Make time to read, watch, and listen to them. Stand under the night sky, reflecting on your heroes.

6. Connect with LIFE. Life is a force beyond emotion. Connect with the miracle of your heartbeat, grass growing in a sidewalk crack, and bird migrations. The cycles of life and death are humbling and inspiring.

7. Connect with NOW – focus all your attention on one sense, such as seeing, hearing, touch. Or, focus all your senses on one action—sight, smell, taste, sound, and texture—as you take a bite of food or a sip of tea. My favorite is savoring a cup of tea from a beautifully glazed pottery mug—using herbs I grew in my garden. It connects me with Earth, the seasons, others' artisanry, and my own senses. Evidence shows that intentional breathing, or being intently aware of the senses, done for 12 minutes a day for 8 weeks, can rewire our nervous system, allowing us to live with greater wisdom.

8. Connect with your Life Purpose –When you clearly understand and describe your purpose, you can prioritize your time and energy and are more likely to feel fulfilled and satisfied. You can create a life you love.

Conclusion

I started writing this chapter with the thought of the polarity between art and science, right brain & left brain, and Eastern and Western religious and health systems. As I immersed myself in the essence of heart whispers and heart wisdom I returned to a place of balance recognizing that they don't exist independent of each other. Our heart has a right side and a left side, it works as a whole. When we combine the wisdom of both we get a synergy. My artist mother uses geometry and science to create balance and proportion when she paints. My scientist dad was inspired by the love and beauty of the earth to dedicate his life to helping others be able to access natural environments. I wish each of you the JOY of connecting with and living from your unique heart whispers.

ABOUT THE AUTHOR: Dr. Sharon Montes, MD, is an internationally recognized pioneer in the field of integrative health and holistic medicine. For three decades, she has served as Medical Director for prestigious healthcare facilities such as The University of Maryland Center for Integrative Medicine, the University of Colorado - Rose and AF Williams Family Medicine Centers, and North Texas Area Arlington Community Health Center. Her commitment is to help spiritually-oriented community leaders serve with greater health, joy, and freedom. Her passion and purpose are focused on offering Living Well Positive Intelligence Coaching Programs to help people upgrade their personal operating system to live with health, happiness, and efficiency.

Sharon Montes MD
livingwellwholehealth.com/PQ
support@livingwellwholehealth.com
970-682-4885

CHAPTER 7

The Journey to Happiness and All Things Like It

Nicole C. Carey

Have you ever had a moment where you question everything you've been doing, and—despite success and the outward trappings of a good life—continue to feel unfulfilled, incomplete, not good enough? Well, I've had hundreds, if not thousands, of those moments. In fact, since childhood, something inside was longing for something more than what I was experiencing and what I felt. My inner thoughts went something like this: *This can't possibly be all that my life is supposed to be about, can it? Why do I feel like I am not my whole self? Why don't I feel more joy? Why do I feel incomplete? Why do I feel like I am playing small in life and not truly expressing who I really am?* Day after day, night after night, those questions went through my head over and over, as if I was an over-caffeinated hamster stuck on a spinning wheel.

You know what I did about it for much of my life? Absolutely nothing. I got caught up in day-to-day survival mode and focused on externally driven desires: success in school, my career and relationships, and acquiring "stuff." I glossed over and stuffed down pain and any hint of negative emotion, weakness, and vulnerability in my relentless attempt to create a picture-perfect life—to find what I thought "happy" was supposed to look like. I was pretty darn good at it too, but what I achieved never felt "enough" or created happiness for very long. Then, one day, I couldn't ignore the inner voice any longer. But, believe me, I tried.

My story is not one of linear spiritual progression. It is a story of a winding road where I took three steps forward and ten steps back, where I got lost, got turned around, and had to course correct. I've been stuck on the side of the road, not for just days or weeks, but sometimes years. It involves wanting something, and then forgetting or getting distracted, and wanting something, and then forgetting and being distracted again. My consciousness journey has been about often getting caught up in my own head, second-guessing myself, and being stuck as surely as if I was standing in cement. And yet, that heart and soul stirring inside of me always came back, calling for me to pay attention and listen. And, once it's activated, there's no going back.

For much of my life I was never a religious or spiritual person; in fact, when planning my wedding I explicitly stated that the word God was not to be included in the ceremony. God, religion, and faith were things that people created to give their lives meaning and structure in a world of chaos and uncertainty. And my belief about what happens after you die? Game over. We're worm food. I did believe that we are all energy, and that there was some inexplicable interconnection between human beings and nature. Those things made logical sense to me, and that logic was the lens through which I viewed life.

The journey to awakening my heart and connecting to Self and the Universe began in graduate school. I took a Landmark Forum seminar on personal development and quickly realized that I didn't know my ass from my elbow. It made me question my life, relationships, and purpose. It opened me to synchronicity and serendipity. It ignited in me an expanded questioning and longing. I wanted to understand why despite having so many great things

Chapter 7
The Journey to Happiness and All Things Like It

in my life I felt unfulfilled and incomplete. I wanted to understand why so much crap happened to me and if there was a way to stop it. I wanted to understand the greater wisdom of the Universe and how I fit into it. I began to have deeper, introspective conversations and was drawn to certain books like James Redfield's *The Celestine Prophecy*. I had a burning desire to know if I was on my right path and what my higher purpose was.

And then I got distracted with life, learning, and love for many years. I went into hyper-achievement mode and God and the Universe took a backseat. It wasn't until a miscarriage at the age of thirty-three that I found myself asking a higher intelligence for help. I was the CEO of a nonprofit and living my best life when during a business lunch I felt something was wrong. In an instant, my world came crashing down. Feeling adrift, unsupported, and like my body had betrayed me, I lay under the covers in my dark room, wanting to be alone and yet wanting someone or something to surround me, soothe me, and end my self-loathing and suffering. My heart wasn't whispering. It cried in agony.

That pregnancy loss was the tipping point. I truly cracked open. My heart and my inner listening cracked open. My journey to reconnect with my deeper self and universal intelligence was reignited. Yet, from that point forward, my life did not follow a straight trajectory toward full heart awakening or enlightened consciousness in the body. Oh, how I wish it did! Like most of us seeking the meaning and purpose of our lives, I wanted to press some existential "easy" button and get there. But that's not how life works.

If I am being honest, the reason it didn't work that way for me is because I'm fundamentally stubborn. I have not known how to get out of my own head, and certainly not out of my own way. As much as I would love to blame God, my stepfather, my parents, my former husband, bosses, healers, and so on, the root cause of my greatest triumphs and tragedies always comes back to me.

What happened next? I threw myself full force into work but also engaged a spiritual healer for guidance and support. Three years later, I had my daughter. And, like the Grinch whose heart expanded three sizes, my heart exploded with love for this little being I had been so scared to receive. Through her, I experienced an unfathomable well of unconditional love and connection with my own heart. She was my greatest awakener and continues to be my greatest teacher to this day. But, let's just say some of those lessons have gone down hard.

Again, I wish I could say that having my daughter was my equivalent to pressing that button, that once she was born everything miraculously became amazingly clear and easy. Alas, this was not the case. I think the reason our hearts expand after having children is that we need that expansion to face the challenges of daily life as a parent. As much as I've tried to advance spiritually, my daughter is a continuous reminder that I am still all too human and imperfect.

Yet, as I moved forward in my spiritual progression, I began to realize how I continued to block my full expression—and let my ego cover my pain, wounds, and fears—and trying to maintain the façade of a perfect human and spiritual being. Yet, I never felt like I was enough and fully worthy of love; I lived in a perpetual state of exhaustion and unworthiness. It manifested in debilitating Lyme disease, a second miscarriage, and chronic thyroid issues. I spent years working and writing with a healer and mentor only to see that relationship end. I endured watching my child suffer from unexpected and unspeakable circumstances that made me question God, my own sanity, and my ability to survive and love. I also chose to end my marriage after twenty-seven years. And this was all while on my "awakened" spiritual path. None of that makes me unique—it simply makes me human.

Through all of it, I tried to meditate, journal, repeat mantras and

Chapter 7
The Journey to Happiness and All Things Like It

affirmations, listen to spiritual music, follow my breath, change my diet, and be more conscious of my thoughts and actions. Sometimes it worked. Often, I got caught up in life and those practices got pushed off my "to-do list." At one particularly rough period, I learned the pleasure of Core Energetics, where I spent sixty minutes every few weeks hitting a plastic bat on a huge foam block and screaming things that I could never say to anyone. The safety of that teacher and that space to be imperfect got me through some tough moments.

I am living proof that you can do things the easy way or the hard way. Sometimes I've chosen the hard way. (Actually, most times). I have had this story in my head that things must be hard to be true, real, or worthwhile. I believed it was through the greatest pain that I would reap the greatest gain. My life would've been so much easier if I realized sooner that our beliefs and thinking determine our reality and experiences. My life did not and does not have to be so hard and I have the power to change it.

I've finally learned to stop screwing around and focus on the things that really matter to me. It's taken a swift spiritual kick in the ass from a series of channeled non-physical beings, known as the Jeshua Collective, to finally snap me to full attention. I call it my spiritual "scared straight" moment. I realized that what I have been wanting all along is my own direct connection and ability to hear and speak with Source. I want to be a direct channel. Why learn to channel? Because it provides me with direct guidance from Source on how to live my best life. Because it is the very best way to receive energy work and healing. Because it finally puts me in the driver's seat of my own Source connection.

For much of my life, I felt I needed other spiritual leaders, healers, intuitives, and psychics to tell me what I needed to do or what Source wanted to share with me. I thought the spiritual growth I was feeling and receiving over the years was mostly due to working with others' spiritual capacities rather than my own. I didn't trust my intuition, my inner connection, or the knowing and feelings inside of me. I now realize I have a direct connection with spiritual intelligence (God, Source, or universal energy—whatever you choose to call it). I also have a non-physical support team whose sole purpose is to help guide and coach me through life. Who knew?!

Joy, love, happiness, power, and the greater truths of the Universe are my birthright—I just didn't realize it until recently. I just didn't choose it. And despite my spiritual inferiority complex, I, like everyone, have the capacity for direct connection with higher intelligence and All That Is. And how I need to get there is way easier than I've made it.

A few minutes of meditation each day has made all the difference (truthfully, just twelve minutes in the morning). If I had consistently done that earlier, I could've saved myself years and years of grief. I've learned a quieted mind creates the ability to learn from your Higher Self and Guides. If I had just taken those few minutes to get out of my head I would've heard and listened to the calling of my heart and soul and the wisdom of my guide team more clearly. I now know that they were always singing to me, but I never slowed down enough, and I wasn't quiet or aligned enough inside, to hear the music. Meditation and channeling classes from the Jeshua Collective have changed everything. The moment I chose to consistently mediate and join classes, my abilities and listening opened. I just had to say yes to it. It's taken me over fifty years to get here, but I am finally where I want and need to be.

Perhaps I am a bit of a spiritual late bloomer, and that's A-OK. I *am* a perfect spiritual work in progress. I've also finally realized that my next great life goal has nothing to do with outward material success. It has everything to do with opening a clean, clear, accurate direct connection with my inner guide team and Source energy as an expert trance channel. (Sshh, don't tell my day job). No award, business success, or external validation can ever, will ever, or should

Chapter 7
The Journey to Happiness and All Things Like It

ever replace that inner relationship, connection, and alignment. That's my real #relationshipgoal.

Today, I'm finally listening and living more in the direction of my heart and soul. I am finally headed on a clearer pathway back home to my whole inner self. I have awakened my direct connection with the higher intelligence of my guide team through channeling classes. And, as I continue to work to "get there," I'm enjoying my journey so much more. I'm saying yes to happiness and all things like it more. I am saying yes to greater joy, ease, and abundance. Importantly, I am enjoying being a highly intuitive, source connected, and far more joyful business leader, mentor, mom, human, and spiritual being. And whatever comes from all that is *perfect*.

ABOUT THE AUTHOR: Nicole Carey is an award-winning business executive with nearly thirty years working and leading teams within government, non-profit, and for-profit agencies. She currently serves as a Chief Strategy Officer specializing in government management and strategic advisory services. She is an intrepid life navigator, seeker of truth, awakening channel, and trail blazer trying to discover a better pathway to Source-connected living and business success. She is a business and empowerment coach and mentor committed to helping all people, especially women, thrive and find their version of happiness and all things like it.

Nicole Carey
Business and Empowerment Coach
nicoleccarey.com
nicoleccarey@gmail.com
240-389-0894

CHAPTER 8

Fall Seven Times and Stand Up Eight Times
"七転八起"

Tsuki Imie

There is a Japanese proverb, "Nana korobi ya oki," which means, "Fall down seven times, stand up eight."

In life, everyone stumbles in some way or another, and I am no exception. I can now express my heart in this way and would like to send words of support to those who, like me, have almost given up on life many times. They follow a glimmer of light out of the darkness, sometimes slipping back into it, and so on, until they are finally able to step out into the public eye and begin to walk again. Light—darkness—new light, even brighter.

This has been the story of my life: moving on, despite hitting several obstacles, right up to the present. I was born and raised in Japan, and after graduating from college I became an "OL"—or "Office Lady/Secretary"—at a pharmaceutical company in 1986. I felt uncomfortable in my own skin and kept myself small at work, just going through the motions needed to complete my tasks. Working in that company, I felt I was doing what was expected from my family and upbringing; however, I eventually found myself thinking back to the dreams I had in childhood. I even looked at my diary from kindergarten, and it felt as if I were going back in time. I realized I had forgotten who I was as a child. At the time, I remained focused on my career and told myself I did not have time to look back on the past, but I couldn't help it—especially when I found hidden in my diary a picture and a sentence that I had written at four years old: ''I will go abroad one day.''

Four years later, in the spring of 1990, I had the opportunity to attend college in Utah, and I took it. Everything was new and exciting, and I must admit I enjoyed going out and having fun more than studying. Interestingly, it wasn't until I returned to Japan that I met and fell in love with an American man. I went back to America with him, this time to California. As I look back, it was like rolling up the second chapter of a book. Another four years passed in the blink of an eye, and I had an opportunity to do something new, something I never considered before: I would attend a culinary school.

I thought, *Well, I'll become a cook and try it out for a few years.* However, what first felt like a whim soon turned into a serious pursuit. I worked diligently to achieve perfection and push forward toward my new dream of being a chef. I kept making mistakes but kept learning more and advancing in my career. During this time, I also married without my parents' permission. I didn't tell them for two years because I knew my mother disapproved of this man. Sure enough, when I finally told them of the marriage, they disowned me. Still, I continued to move forward. I focused on becoming a chef and being financially independent.

Though I achieved my professional goals, my marriage went in another direction. After fourteen years, I knew I needed to forgive him but also to move on without him. I had known all along that I needed to be independent, and maybe that's why I worked so hard to become a chef. Now an Executive Sous Chef at a hotel, I was working, even on my days off, to pay for my divorce lawyer. My parents knew that I was having a rough time and told me ''You

Chapter 8
Fall Seven Times and Stand Up Eight Times

don't have to stay there anymore, just come back to Japan." I felt I hit the wall again. I felt shame because I had married my American husband without their permission. Still, I thought, *No matter what the circumstances, I should not give up and leave the U.S.A.* Despite the stressful circumstances, I was able to make a living on my own. I also carved out the time to relax, focus on myself, and regain confidence in who I was.

As one chapter closes another chapter opens. While dealing with divorce, I had a reading done by a psychic who told me I would be with someone I already knew. "He has two children," she said, then repeated that I had already met him. I still laugh when I think about it because I already did know Mark, but at the time I didn't like him at all! Then, one day, things changed. I realized Mark was my soul mate and best friend; I also realized I had pictured him all those years ago back in kindergarten. He was part of my dream for my future even then.

Life was new and exciting again as we explored each other's lives. Strangely enough, something inside me became more "sensitive" and was able to express itself outwardly and organically. This was a big change that would affect me more than I had imagined.

I felt I had clairsentience in the past, but now I was feeling it stronger and more clearly than before. Like many people, Mark was skeptical of such things…until the evening of March 10. We were sitting on the sofa together when I suddenly turned to Mark and said, "I'm feeling an earthquake." Mark looked around the apartment and said, "We're not having one—nothing is moving or swinging." The next morning we woke up to the news of an earthquake in Japan. I can't explain why or how this worked, it was just something I could sense.

I also had begun warning Mark not to cross the street at a particular intersection—if he did, he was going to get run over by a car or truck. For weeks, I said this to him. His reaction, as always, was to not take it seriously. One day, when he was crossing that street, in that spot, a truck ran through the light, almost hitting him. Another example occurred prior to my surgery for a shoulder injury sustained in a skiing accident. I felt the need to tell and prepare him, saying things like, "Do you know where to call if something happens to me?" and "How much life insurance would you get?"

"Again with that?" he said. "It's a simple one-day surgery and you're overthinking it."

He wouldn't listen to me. Every day, for ten days before the surgery, I said the same thing to him, and each day he dismissed it. Well, after that "simple surgery," something went wrong. I lost a lot of blood and my blood pressure dropped into the thirties! I remember asking Mark to leave because I didn't want him to see me die. I lost consciousness in the emergency room and had my own experience of hovering between life and death. I kept thinking and saying, "I have so much more to do, I can't go now." He said there was a rush of activity going into the emergency room and after an hour he was allowed back to see me. After that he couldn't doubt it anymore. He had experienced my knowing firsthand.

That was in 2019. Life was good. I had Mark and I was established and satisfied with my work. I was a Corporate Chef at the company's headquarters. I cooked for the Japanese Prime Minister, as well as the Japanese Emperor when he was in the U.S. Then things changed abruptly. Sometimes things get twisted and can't be explained—all I can say is that thinking about it, even now, makes me feel physically shaken and humiliated. Because of this incident, I was identified as mentally disabled from June 2019 to June 2021. For these years I had depression, anxiety, PTSD, and psychosis. I couldn't walk, I was afraid of people, couldn't go outside, couldn't drive a car, couldn't think for myself, couldn't remember, couldn't stand, couldn't accept food, and had ringing in my ears, delusions, and hallucinations. I sleepwalked; I resented

Chapter 8
Fall Seven Times and Stand Up Eight Times

everyone. No one could have predicted that I, who had led a such smooth-sailing life, would fall so badly!

I didn't even know who I was.

At the time, medications and treatments were changing so rapidly that it seemed as if I was being experimented on. No medicine worked for me, and a few of my therapists gave up on me and said, "I don't know if you can be cured." One therapist even said, "You are not making any effort to get better, and you are intentionally making yourself feel trapped mentally." I had no one to turn to and I felt everything was against me. During these years, I almost gave up living.

One morning in 2019, as soon as I woke up, I told Mark, ''I don't know why, but I see I will do tarot readings. Maybe I will be a healer one day."

"What a busy morning," Mark replied—a typical reaction when I said something weird. No way could someone who had spent more than twenty-five years as a chef suddenly become a healer! I had never even touched a tarot card, and now I was going to be a tarot reader? On the other hand, no one could have imagined that I would have had such a horrible time after all my success. The years of mental lapses, health problems, and the most painful of all, the mental disability, had led to a greater determination to move forward. What I am about to share with you is what I mentioned at the beginning of this chapter. And I would be more than happy if you could share it with your friends and family and let it be a source of emotional support for you.

At that time, a fate appraiser suggested I do Reiki, saying, "You will have a mission as a healer from now on. Now I can say to you, welcome to the world of healers.''

Again, I was reminded of my past. I remembered when I said, ''Well, it looks like I will be a healer in the future, like doing tarot readings.'' I had said it to Mark, and now it was coming back to me.

I was still struggling with my desperation, but I thought I would try anyway. My head was still fuzzy and foggy; I couldn't remember, I couldn't concentrate, and yet I knew that one day something would change, that *I would be able to change.*

Over the next two years, I got certified as a Reiki Master and began providing sessions to acquaintances; I also did tarot readings. It was a great way to recover myself. Still, I was slow to speak, weak in thought, and often dazed. One day, I did a Reiki session with my friend whose energy was stagnant in the upper part of her body, diffusing the energy toward her legs. As I focused on that energy blockage, I felt a vibration in my stomach area, along with a tremor throughout my body. At that moment, the fog in my head quickly lifted. It is very difficult to describe, but it was amazing! Immediately following the session, the way I spoke, the speed at which I spoke, and even the pitch of my voice changed. For a moment I thought, *Who is that? 'Who am I? The old me? A new me?* I wasn't sure, but I was relieved and happy! That night, Mark recognized my changes. "I don't know what happened to you today," he said, "but welcome back." I knew I still had to be diligent, I still had to make up for those "lost" five years, but I would thrive!

Now I know that people experience falls when they don't intend it and least expect it. And, without recognition, sometimes people rise. When people overcome hardship, they find out life's purposes.

And here I am: Reiki Healer, tarot and oracle card reader, medium, therapist, and more to come!

ABOUT THE AUTHOR: Tsuki Imie is an intuitive, healer, and entrepreneur based in San Diego. After twenty-seven years in the culinary industry, Tsuki left her position as Corporate Menu Design Chef to focus on her spiritual gifts. She studied Reiki under William Lee Rand, who follows the lineage of Hawayo Takata, Chujiro Hayashi, and Mikao Usui. Today, in addition to Reiki, Tsuki

Chapter 8
Fall Seven Times and Stand Up Eight Times

offers tarot and oracle readings, psychic mediumship readings, Bio Lymphatic Drainage Therapy, Spiritual Response Therapy, Chakra tooth gems, and healthy cooking classes. Her passion is promoting relaxation, stress reduction, and healthy alternatives for daily living. Sessions are held on her fifty-foot vessel on San Diego Bay.

Tsuki Imie
Total Wellness by Tsuki Imie
tsukiimie.com
tsukiimie@gmail.com
858-525-5113

CHAPTER 9

Turning Points

Ordinary Days Can Lead to Major Life Shifts

Sue Campanella

I swore I would never get divorced. When I was about ten, my parents embarked on a traumatic divorce that lasted about three years; this was the first turning point in my life. I made a promise to myself then, that if I ever decided to get married and have kids I would NEVER divorce and do that to my children.

Though I didn't realize it until later, adolescence and young adulthood were driven by anger at having been traumatized by my parents' submergence into their drama with each other. That anger hidden inside me, combined with my youth, would result in my being attracted to a man who was often the life of the party. Everyone thought he was great. Reality was, he was fighting demons worse than mine. I was nineteen when we met; we moved in together about three months later, just before my twentieth birthday; and we married at twenty-three. The natural progression after that was to buy a house and start a family, which we did, three years later when my daughter was born.

The first night home from the hospital I woke up for the two-a.m. feeding. It felt like the world was asleep, that my daughter and I were the only people on the planet. The love that I had for this child, an unconditional love I never dreamt possible, was intoxicating. This was another turning point in my life. I realized then that being married to the "life of the party" was not going to be enough for myself or my child. This is when I began to realize that my life had to shift, I had to find my truth, my voice. I had to heal that inner child who was so traumatized and disappointed, who felt unloved and unlovable. Yet the promise I had made to my ten-year-old self was ingrained in my psyche. The birth of my second daughter was another turning point—one that would lead to several others that completely changed my life.

First, I finally summoned the courage to break that promise. This allowed me to forge my own path, not the path family and friends expected me to continue. This courage also allowed me to unexpectedly meet an amazing man who, even to this day, loves me more than anyone in my life ever has. Feeling loved—dare I say, adored—by my current husband gave me the confidence and motivation to begin to find ways to heal myself, to love myself. The question—how, and where do I start?

Motivation and love by themselves do not overcome negative mind chatter. I learned how to be more in the present moment, which opened to the next turning point. The *Celestine Prophecy,* which was shared with me by a close friend, opened my mind, heart, and soul to how tapping into and trusting Divine Power can change your life, your mindset, even your health. This began my understanding of how connected our bodies and mind truly are, how we are not our parents, siblings, or ancestors. We are unique, as are our journeys.

Hungry for more information and my true connectedness, I became obsessed with reading books to gain more knowledge. I would simply walk the metaphysical rows of a local bookstore and allow myself to be drawn to a specific book. What I thought was just curiosity, I now realize, was my purpose, my passion, my reason to be on this planet at this time, having gone through the

Chapter 9
Turning Points

experiences I had been through.

The next turning point was in the form of our unpopular decision to move our family from Rhode Island to Florida. This really tested my resolve to find my truth. Our family and friends couldn't understand why we would move away. My father actually promised my youngest daughter that he would buy her a horse (she was taking horseback riding lessons at the time) if she would make a stink to stay in Rhode Island! "Mom guilt" set in, along with the negative mind chatter that said, "Have I just ruined my kids' lives by moving them fourteen hundred miles from everything and everyone they know and love?" Yet at the same time, I had a mission to move out of state and start fresh. There were negative energies compromising me and my family in Rhode Island. I later realized this mission was my inner voice, my higher self, guiding me to my truth and purpose, allowing my shift in energy to help shift my family's as well. Sometimes you have to be uncomfortable before you can find your peace.

Once in Florida, I took a sales position at a local newspaper. This job required me to cold call businesses in my territory. One beautiful, highly memorable day, I drove into a strip mall with the intent to cold call and noticed a business called Sacred Space. Intrigued, I walked up to the door, put my hand on the handle, and pushed it open. As one foot stepped inside, a feeling came over me—this was no advertising call, but something for me, personally. Once again, I didn't realize at the time, that this was my higher self guiding me to another turning point toward my path of purpose and empowerment.

I noticed a stunning array of crystals, gemstones, books, jewelry, and items that I wasn't familiar with. This storefront had an inviting scent and energy to it. There was a lovely woman standing behind the counter, so I walked up, said hello, and asked what Sacred Space was all about. She was the mom of Lani, the owner, and proudly gave me a little tour. It just so happened they were having a psychic fair the next day and she invited me to come. She was excited for me to meet Lani and the other healers that would be there. I had never been to a psychic fair before and was intrigued, excited, and a little nervous. I went home and told my husband and two teenage daughters, but no one shared my excitement. I didn't even understand it myself.

When I returned to Sacred Space the next day I was met with the same calming scent and energy. There were quite a few people there, along with a menu of different healings. New to this, I had no idea what I needed. I was guided by a very friendly woman to have a cord-cutting and DNA activation. WOW! The energy I felt, the love I felt around me, was something I had never experienced before. I didn't quite understand what they did, and what it would mean for me, but I went home in such a blissful state, I knew I wanted more!

The next day, my husband and I went to the beach. We went there often, but on this day the beauty of the beach was magnified tremendously. It was like a veil had lifted from my eyes, my heart, my soul. I remember walking down the beach mesmerized by the way the sun glistened off the water just so. The amazing blue of the Gulf of Mexico, the color and texture of the sand. I kept saying to my husband, "Can you see it? Can you see how amazingly beautiful it is today? Is it just me? Can you see it too?" He answered flatly, "Yeah, it's beautiful," with that strange look like, it's the same beach we always go to, what's different about it today? *I* was different, and had taken another validating step in my journey.

The healings I was receiving shifted my energy and allowed me to attract what was in my highest good. An ordinary day at the soccer field turned into another turning point. I was sitting by myself watching my daughter play when a mom from the opposing team asked if she could place her chair by mine. We struck up a conversation. She began to tell me how she practices energy

Chapter 9
Turning Points

medicine. Using kinesiology, or muscle testing, she asked the body what it needed. I was beyond intrigued and booked a session with her. This was life-changing, and not just because of the healing my body received. I was so drawn to this line of work that enabled healing physically, emotionally, mentally, and spiritually. If only I could do what she did, but how?

There was a nagging feeling in my brain. "Help people be who they were born to be before all the programming" became a mantra in my mind. I wasn't even sure what that meant or how it could be accomplished but those words would not leave my mind.

Sitting home alone one day, I was flipping through the TV channels and found the movie *Under the Tuscan Sun*. I had wanted to see it in the theater but never had the chance, or so I thought. After watching the movie, I realized I wasn't in a place in my journey to see it when it first came out, but I now was ready. If you are unfamiliar with the film, it's about a woman, played by Diane Lane, who gets a divorce she is not expecting and goes to Italy to start a new life. She wants to buy a home and start a family. Things don't turn out exactly as she had planned. It was the very end of the movie that sparked another turning point. There was a wedding going on at Diane Lane's character's property. She was standing on the hillside looking down at the festivities, feeling sorry for herself. Her friend came up to her and said, "Everything you wanted has happened." She was shocked at this remark. Then he began to show her what was really in front of her. How she'd built this beautiful home with strangers who were now family. Her best friend had even joined her in Italy to have her own baby, and her home was truly a home of love and laughter. For the main character, this was a light bulb moment—and it was for me too!

Everything was right in front of me—all the work I had been doing, the relationships I formed with like-minded people. My journey had led me to the realization that now was the time to really take action, to "Just Do It," as Nike says.

My research into the "how-to" of this new chapter of my life led me to become certified as a Life Coach. I was determined to be "all-in," so with the support of my husband I quit my well-paying sales job. Talk about a turning point! Yet the fear, self-doubt, and questions like, "What have I done to my family's finances? Am I being selfish?" went around in my mind like a broken record.

The decision was made, there was no turning back. What does one do? Bring out all the tools that have been learned over the years and release what no longer serves you! It was terrifying, but exhilarating. This is what it is like to live your truth. The joy, passion, and confidence this work gave me was something I had never felt before. I started a monthly Goddess Circle where people could discuss issues that were not serving them and I could teach them tools to overcome fear, anxiety, low self-esteem, et cetera. From those classes I gained clients and my business began to grow. My confidence was growing too, as was my knowledge. I was introduced to Reiki and felt this would be a great tool to help me and my clients. I soon became a Reiki Master. Though I could quiet my mind more quickly and easily than before, the self-doubt still swirled. I asked myself things like, "Who do you think you are?" and "You are just Sue Campanella, why do you think you can help make such change in peoples' lives?" But I was! The feedback I was getting from clients was amazing. "Words of Wisdom" were coming out of my mouth that surprised even me! When clients asked me to repeat what I had just said so they could write it down, I really couldn't. They were not my words, I was being guided as to what my clients needed. Amazing!

More modalities were added to my lineup, but the turning point was the Emotion and Body Code. This modality enabled me to truly help people be who they were born to be before the programming set in. Like my soccer mom friend, I was now able to help people heal

Chapter 9
Turning Points

their bodies, mind, and spirit. Today I am living my truth through my work. I have partnered with physicians who understand that it takes a village for true healing to occur. I would not change any part of my journey, and I'm grateful to all those who have participated in my challenges and my growth. They are why I am where I am today, filled with joy and looking forward to more healing tomorrow. That little girl at the beginning of this story is very proud of the woman she grew up to be. She now realizes how brave she was to break the promise to herself. She not only broke the promise, she broke the generational cycle of guilt, self-doubt, and physical ailment, allowing her to help others do the same.

ABOUT THE AUTHOR: Sue Campanella, Reiki Master, and owner of Transformations Life Coaching & Healing, LLC, has a mission to enable clients to "Be the YOU, you were born to be." Sue uses modalities such as The Emotion and Body Codes to release imbalances that are causing physical pain, emotional blocks, negative mind chatter, and more. She also serves as her clients' accountability partner, teaching them tools so they can empower themselves and shed what no longer serves them. Sue firmly believes that it takes a village and partners with various physicians to help unlock true healing.

Sue Campanella, CTACC, CECP, CBCP
Transformations Life Coaching & Healing, LLC
tlclifecoaching4u.com
sue@tlclifecoaching4u.com
401-225-1693

CHAPTER 10

Say YES and Hang On!

Amy Budd

I love hearts! I always have. As a kid I sketched them on all my notebooks and had a pair of show chaps for horseback riding with silver heart conchos on the back. I even signed my name with a heart!

Our hearts are truly amazing on so many levels. Our physical heart is a fantastic muscle, pumping over two thousand gallons of blood throughout our body each day. The heart is the first organ formed in utero, long before our brain develops. Our hearts also have a profound spiritual component. It is my belief that our physical heart can connect us to our energetic or spiritual heart. Our spiritual heart can be our "guiding light" when we learn how to listen to, utilize, and flex that muscle!

Most of us use that guidance, that inner knowing, our higher self, more frequently than we recognize. We fall in love, we adopt pets, we make friends, we follow hunches—that is the heart whispering. We seem to struggle, however, when it comes to our purpose or life path. We hesitate, we question, we don't always listen or trust our hearts. We allow our logical brain to take over and talk us into—or, sometimes, out of—those bigger life decisions.

I am at an age where it is easier to look in the rear-view mirror, see my path, and recognize that I have been following my heart far longer than I realized. My hope with this story is to empower people to recognize and follow their heart whispers at a much younger age, allow yourself to become that bigger version, and do the work you were meant to do here for a longer period of time.

My First Big YES

My own story starts with wanting to be a veterinarian. I came out of the womb animal-crazy. If Dr. Doolittle and Dr. James Harriot could have a love child, it would be me. I started campaigning for a horse when I was four or five years old. My parents divorced when I was two, so having a single, schoolteacher mom, I knew owning a horse would not be a possibility. So, I spent hours as a young kid pretending I was a horse. I had a blue Windtamer jacket I would put on, pull the hood up tight around my face, and "gallop" around the front yard. Then I would run to the front porch and eat my oats (dried oatmeal) out of a bowl.

Thankfully, my mom did remarry when I was ten. For my twelfth birthday I was given four riding lessons. The horse I rode was an American Saddlebred show horse named Chief's Stonewall Pride, or Pride as he was known in the barn. He was the grandest thing I had ever seen. Magically, on the fourth lesson, I learned he was for sale! After many hours of begging and pleading, my parents agreed to the horse, with conditions. I was borrowing the money for the purchase price and had to be able to pay his board for the year. I said yes, yes, yes! I was twelve—you don't know what you don't know. We bought the horse, my stepdad helped me secure commercial mowing jobs, and my fairytale began. Pride was my whole world and the only thing that kept me sane through mean girls in high school, my stepdad's drinking and verbal abuse, the move to a new high school my junior year, an eating disorder, and the trauma of seeing a young man intentionally hit by a car. Pride

Chapter 10
Say YES and Hang On!

was my safe harbor for my heart, my "heart horse" as many people say in the horse world. When I lost him to a freak illness during my sophomore year of college, I buried myself in work and school hoping to escape the pain. Thankfully, a dear friend gathered me up one night, said it was time to move on, and took me out to the local bar to go dancing. That is the night I met my future husband.

I STILL Love Pink!

I finished college, got married, moved to Cheyenne, Wyoming, and decided that before investing four more years in vet school I'd better "try it on" first by working in a clinic. I recognize now, that was a heart whisper. Naively, I'd thought working in a clinic would be all fluffy puppies and kittens. Instead, it was a monumental amount of death and dying. I worked in several different small animal clinics following my husband's career path. When we moved to Denver, I had a clinic job waiting for me. We were getting settled in our home and I got a phone call from a local Mary Kary consultant asking for someone else. I politely informed her she had the wrong number, and, oh, by the way, I don't wear makeup. She was persistent and offered me a complimentary manicure. I looked down at my nails, which were always a mess from taking care of our two horses, and said yes.

As she was doing my nails, Vicki, the Mary Kay consultant, started telling me about the "career opportunity." I was only half-listening until she started talking about the earning potential and how you can impact other women's lives. She also informed me that the company typically looked for—thirty-five- to forty-year-old corporate women who had hit the glass ceiling. This was the '80s, and I was in my twenties working in a veterinary clinic—definitely not the typical "pink lady." Yet I found myself asking Vicki if she would help me.

My heart hurt working in a veterinary clinic and I knew I needed to try something new. When I told him about the opportunity my husband was relieved. No more fostering and rescuing animals! My family was devastated—they thought I was wasting my college education. I was at peace and excited to try a new path.

I had an amazing journey. I earned two cars and had over three hundred customers, as well as sixty consultants in thirteen states. I learned more about myself, working with and developing people, and running my own business than I could have ever imagined. Mary Kay Ash was a true visionary, providing an environment for women to grow, thrive, and succeed. She was my first exposure to limitless thinking.

My husband and I had our first child and made another move to northern Colorado to be closer to family. We purchased a larger property and got an additional horse that could ultimately be the "kid horse." That's when my world slowly started to unravel. My husband reunited with college friends—and resumed the college drinking. With the new baby, I was not able to maintain production standards and keep my Mary Kary car and my unit, so I resigned my directorship thinking that would provide the time I needed to keep things going at home.

Cue the Horses!

Shortly after having my second child, a longtime friend reached out and encouraged me to go to a Linda Tellington-Jones TTouch® clinic for starting young horses. It was perfect timing, as I was feeling so lost, and living in a quiet hell. When I called my mom and told her that I "needed" to go to this clinic, she immediately offered to stay with my kids. My husband was not happy to have his mother-in-law there for a week, but, again, I knew I needed to go. My heart was calling me back to the horses.

Chapter 10
Say YES and Hang On!

The clinic was transformative. At the time there was so much abuse in the horse world. The TTouch method provided a completely different approach. It was about trust, building confidence in both horse and human, and true cooperation. I was hooked! I thought I had found my calling. I spent a couple of years attending clinics and getting certified as a TTouch practitioner and, later, a Centered Riding® Instructor. What I didn't realize at the time was how much my heart was changing and expanding. My spiritual journey was beginning to unfold.

With two little people, three horses, a huge dog, and three cats, the dam finally broke. We had a picture-perfect life from the outside—a nice house, pretty barn, great jobs, kids—but my heart could no longer stay in the marriage. The journey of divorce could be its own story, one of relief, devastation, fear, sadness, and grief rolled into a giant bundle. Divorce brought my whole life into question, and my heart had the answers. Thankfully, I listened.

I moved my kids, then two and five, and the animal crew to Albuquerque, New Mexico. I had a great support network with the TTouch® community, who helped me get set up with local horse people, as well as support from my parents, who also relocated to Albuquerque.

Sweet Treats Change Everything

As my kids got older it became increasingly more difficult to make the horse work fit into a manageable schedule. On a whim, I made homemade horse treats for all my clients. Little did I know they would turn out to be affectionately called "horse crack!" This ended up launching a twenty-five-year run in the pet food industry. It started with the horse treats, then dog cookies, cake mixes for horses, dogs, and cats, and eventually a full line of raw, cooked, and dehydrated foods.

During this journey I had to learn to create, manufacture, label, test, and scale production. I had a cease-and-desist order, a bad business partner, and I closed and started over three times. When I started the third time, I had little capital but was determined to do things my way. I broke with the traditional business model and used both a distributor and sold direct-to-consumer for my products. It was not an easy path, and just as I was getting everything dialed in, I felt the tug to come back to the horses.

By that time, my kids were grown and out on their own. My horses had passed at ages twenty-eight and thirty-four, and I was missing that deep connection to them. I had always wanted to learn to drive a team of horses, so once again for a birthday present my parents gave me driving lessons. Can you see where this is going?? I was always obsessed with Clydesdales, and after a few driving lessons started "shopping" for a new horse. I spent hours online looking at what I call "horse porn." I found a horse—a big, black Clydesdale named Andy, located in Canada. It's hard to describe the feeling of "knowing," but I knew he was my horse. I did the most unthinkable thing in the horse world: I bought him sight unseen and hired a shipper I didn't know to deliver him. It didn't matter. I had found another "heart horse."

I knew about horse therapy for physically disabled people and started doing some research about the different personal growth opportunities. Just as I had when "trying out" being a veterinarian, I decided to try out a weekend workshop before investing in the two years of training. This time it was a great fit, so transformative and healing, that I knew I had to go down this path. My "portfolio career" was finally starting to make sense. My last puzzle piece was here, and I knew I needed to come back to the horses and work in partnership with them to heal hearts and evolve souls.

During Covid, I was able to sell part of my pet food business and

Chapter 10
Say YES and Hang On!

make my dream a reality. Once again, from the outside this made no sense, but to my heart, it made perfect sense. I knew all my past experiences had led me to this choice point. When I fully said YES, it was incredible how quickly everything I needed showed up.

An amazing forty-acre property was available, I found two other Clydesdale horses and was given a sassy pony to join the herd. I discovered HeartMath® in the process of my training certification, which gives humans the tangible "how-to" for what horses know innately.

My work now is about helping humans become more like horses. Horses offer clear, honest communication with no emotional strings attached. Horses know how to be in a balanced, coherent state for maximum efficiency. Horses understand that every herd member matters.

As humans, we have so much potential inside us. We are magnificent beings. Our hearts hold the key to our greatness. Learning to quiet the mind so you can hear your heart whispers is our human journey. I have realized my trauma is not unique, my story is not unique; what is unique is my response. I have always been seeking answers. Answers to life's questions, answers to life's mysteries, answers to why things happen.

I understand now I have listened to my heart for much of my journey. Every time I said YES, doors opened. When I said yes and committed to my heart, things happened exponentially faster.

My favorite quote is:

It's impossible, said pride.
It's risky, said experience.
It's pointless, said reason.
Give it a try, whispered the heart.
~ Author Unknown

Our hearts whisper to us all the time. My desire now is to help people not only recognize but choose to hear those whispers.

ABOUT THE AUTHOR: Amy Budd, founder of Whole Heart Ranch, is a certified HeartMath® Resilience Advantage™ Trainer and Coach, and a certified Equine Facilitated Coach. Amy loves bringing her years of business experience to personal and leadership development, utilizing the emotional intelligence of horses to facilitate change. Amy fully believes animals can both heal and educate humans. Her work on her forty-acre ranch combines working with horses as well as guiding people with the HeartMath® tools to open, heal, listen to, and trust their own hearts. Healing hearts and evolving souls while on the planet is her chosen path and provides great joy.

Amy Budd
Whole Heart Ranch
wholeheartranch.com
Work: 970-888-0820
amy@wholeheartranch.com

CHAPTER 11

When a Whisper Becomes a Roar

Beverly Akhurst

All stories begin as seeds, something unknown and waiting to grow. All heart whispers are ripples that began as disturbances at the surface of our lived experience. Disturbances that do not obey the human construct of time. These ripples are gentle waves that grow and spread from each intrusion into our comfortable existence, from each experience that finds its way past the surface of our movement through time. Some of these upsets meet a threshold that reflects the experience back towards us, from the same source but changed, reminding us of something necessary and true which needs to be discerned by the wisdom of our hearts.

This is one of those stories. It's a whisper that grew to a yell as the ripples of time converged and rebounded back toward me the moment a large boulder was dropped into the deep center of my human experience.

"What do you mean you called an ambulance?" I asked the doctor as I sat in a chair in the soulless little room of my local walk-in clinic. I had simply come for a checkup.

"Your pulse is thirty," he replied. "Your blood pressure is so low I can't even believe you are upright and talking to me."

"That is silly! The hospital is two blocks away. I can walk there if you think I should go."

What he said next made no sense to my brain.

"I'm not letting you out of here until they come. You can't walk, you may not make it."

I was stunned, time slowed, and I became an onlooker to what came next...Within minutes I was in the back of an ambulance with paramedics hooking me up to monitors and firing off questions as they readied to take me those two blocks. Shortly after that, I was being admitted to emergency, then rolled into the dimly lit cardiac unit, its peacefulness interrupted only by the beeping of heart monitors tapping out rhythms of incoherence. As I passed each private bed space, I noted the generous size of each room.

Right! I thought. *Necessary if one was to have a heart attack.* This was followed by, *Can't have anyone distressed or upset here* and *Cripes, everyone must be at least forty years older than me!!!*

I was parked in an oversized, glassed-in room where I could be watched by all the nurses for any sign that I was about to launch myself from this life. Stuck-on patches conveyed messages from every pulse point of my body to monitors inking out ticker tape messages that scrolled their way to the earth. "Your pulse is too low," they said. "Your heartbeats are dumping out an extra forty thousand discordant beats a day, throwing off the music of life. Oh, and butterflies are trying to beat a path from your chest."

Wait—what?! I am not even forty-three!

I phoned my then-partner, who arrived with distress on his face. There had, after all, been a couple of ambulance rides in the previous month, calling into question the ability of my heart to circulate enough energy in the moment.

Our conversation went something like this:

Me: "Hey there, how are you doing?"

Him: "How am *I* doing?! How about you!?"

Chapter 11
When a Whisper Becomes a Roar

Me: "Not very happy, kind of scared, but most of all, tired... so tired!!"

Of course, anyone with any medical or physiological knowledge would have said, "No surprise that you're tired—your heart is not pumping properly!" but all I knew at that moment was that I felt a bone-deep exhaustion.

Nine months earlier, my father had been diagnosed with cancer (later we found out it was pancreatic cancer). One of the healthiest, strongest, most present humans I know went to the hospital because his stomach was bloated and he was having trouble eating. He was admitted that same day to emergency and told he had cancer. Thus began a five-month journey of learning how to navigate the waves caused by such an immense boulder. I thought I was equipped. I am a caregiver at the very core of my being, I had training and experience in so many medical and health scenarios, I was balanced and centered, or so I thought; I have a committed Yoga practice and, damn it, I am good at giving up myself for others (insert the word martyrdom here).

I was the only one of three children living near my parents, so of course I was going to do everything possible. I was in a new relationship with an old acquaintance (part of the many ripples that make up so many stories); two years past a miscarriage; and in a job that, while good, did not feed my heart in any way. Now I was watching the slow exit of my father—five months of an ebbing lifeforce as he started preparing for his birth to the next "loka." Five months of me trying to be present in too many iterations of me: hospital commando, employee, caring girlfriend, trainee and fundraiser for the ride to conquer cancer, and the daughter who would not ask too much of her dying father.

When he passed, I was lost, sad, mad, and exhausted. I am like all of you—I carry the stories of my past as slight weights locked to me, and when the person who carries many of the keys departs we feel like we have been thrown into the deep end with no way to the surface. We forget that copies were made of all the keys.

I didn't stop. I moved in with my partner; I did the two-day bike ride for cancer, I flew back East with my mother to help bury my father's ashes, I went back to work, and then…one ambulance, two ambulances, and three.

Oh, this sleep—beep, beep beep, beep—oh, the soft voices, beep, beep - - beep, beep, oh the dreams….just let me sleep… "Hello, doctor, sure all your students can come in with you." They talk amongst themselves, all of them offering up their suspicions and considerations. What could possibly have put this woman of forty-two in the hospital? She has never had a problem with her heart. They come, they go, they collect ticker tape tallies, and, meanwhile, I sleep.

Then, on the seventh morning, I sit up in bed and stretch. Man, I feel gooood. Beep, beep, beep, beep. Why does the nurse look so confused? Hmmm, there she is on the phone now; boy, am I hungry. I hope someone is going to bring me breakfast! Here comes the doc, gaggle of students in tow.

"Good morning, Beverly. We aren't sure what is going on, but everything is normal." A lot of questions and conversation later, they say, "Well, it all looks normal, but there must be something wrong. I think it must be a flap in your heart, so I think we should do an ablation…."

"A what?"

"An ablation—burn out a piece of your heart. Of course, there is a chance something does go wrong and you may need a pacemaker, but if you were my sister I would tell you to do it."

What!!!?

I convinced them to release me from the hospital with the promise that I would think about the operation. Something about it felt wrong. I had slept for seven days. My heart was getting louder; it

Chapter 11
When a Whisper Becomes a Roar

was nearly screaming at me, "YOU WERE EXHAUSTED! DON'T YOU GET IT??"

It was like unblocking my ears after getting them full of water. The words had been coming from my heart, but I had overwhelmed myself so much with the noise of life I couldn't hear. The whisper had become a roar. What I did not tell the doctor was that I was going to listen to my heart, my gut, my intuition.

I went back to my Yoga practice, which had drifted into my blind spot, and deepened my experience with breath and slower, more conscious movement. Meditation returned not as a thing to do but a needed part of my daily rhythms. I quit my job with the support of the Universe's nudging, took some time to breathe, and fell into my true purpose and passion.

I never did need the operation. The following year, when my heart whispered its next request, I was ready to hear it. *Stop trying to live the way you have been told to,* it said, *you were meant for something so much more. I am so sorry I had to push you into a hospital, but I needed you to hear me, to really stop and hear me. I know you have tried over the years, but so far you have only danced on the periphery of your life. The Ritam is calling you. I am the pulse and the beat of everything you are meant to be and I have waited long enough. It is time.*

With that message pulsing through every cell of me, I picked up a phone, called a Yoga school I knew did regular teacher training and the very next day began to dance a far more rhythmic and sensual dance with my heart.

It is a magical thing that happens once you listen to the whispers and once you choose to trust how to move with the rhythm. It is as if you are being held close by the Source of All Life, cheek to cheek, heart to heart, being guided without force or effort across the skies. At the age of forty-three I became a Yoga teacher and I did not stop, I then opened my own studio, my own teacher training school, hoping to move Yoga into the realm of Ritam (the laws of nature that govern everything of the material world), rather than poses. I started seeing the depth and beauty of everything that creates our beautiful bodies and became a posture and movement specialist, running retreats and guiding workshops.

For my fiftieth birthday, I attended a Yoga festival in Joshua Tree. On the last day, in the middle of a class with two hundred other beautiful beings, I sat up with tears streaming down my face. I had realized that I was madly, deeply, passionately in love with myself.

I am now late into my fifties, sharing my earned elderhood through teaching, coaching, facilitation, storytelling, writing, and podcasts—no longer pushing into a life that was never meant to be mine. I choose to support other women in any way that I can to remove the obstacles that block them from hearing their hearts. This hridya (heart), this dais of our lived experience, carries the whispers from the mind, body, and itself. I used to hear all these whispers when I was young. They were my best friends, my greatest teachers, my guides to the stars. As I let them in now, the pulse of life becomes more rhythmic and a beat that flows through all of life is heard.

I offer you this: listen to the whispers, those gentle, breathy calls that slide past our awareness. Those moments a sweet friend leans in to share their most intimate secrets—you know, the ones that bond you together with the depth of their honesty?

Do I live perfectly now for having heard the whispers? No, but I know when I have stopped listening. I feel the ripples building into crashing waves and then I sit back, take a breath, and ask my heart what I have forgotten. She whispers sweet words back to me and we begin to find our rhythm together again.

Here I am as I come to the end of the story, which is also the beginning as much as it is the middle and everything in between. A short time ago I lost my oldest sister to cancer, the same cancer

Chapter 11
When a Whisper Becomes a Roar

as my father; a new story sends its whispers to my heart, ready to weave itself into the fabric of my being, changing the patterns that briefly highlighted this tapestry, adding beauty, strength, and depth. The whispers have a new urgency. They are no longer just mine but arise from the hearts of those I have known. They are easier and easier to hear now, because I am willing to lean in, be silent, and try to hear the wisdom they share. The rhythm they create is a thing of beauty as they tap out their message, and I wait for the ripples to soften and then return with their new and knowing message.

Don't wait for your whispers to become a roar.

ABOUT THE AUTHOR: Beverly Akhurst is a Yoga teacher, speaker, writer, and owner of Ocean Breath Yoga. Beverly formerly worked in the mental health, education, tech, and travel fields; however, in her early forties, a stay in the cardiac unit began a journey to discover her purpose and the creation of a program she calls Ritam of Life. Beverly is also a student of anatomy and Bhakti Yoga, trained in TRE, and Certified in CranioSacral Therapy. She specializes in posture, movement, and breath and frequently shares her insights through storytelling and on podcasts. Beverly forest bathes whenever she can and believes "It is time we all become the experts of our own lives." She lives in Vancouver.

Beverly Akhurst
Ritam of Life
oceanbreathyoga.ca
oceanbreathyoga@gmail.com
linkedin.com/in/beverly-akhurst-om

CHAPTER 12

Becoming Empowered

Virginia Hunter Sampson

Empowered. I had no idea what that meant and even less of an idea about how to become empowered or if I even *wanted* to become empowered. It sounded kind of scary and "trendy," I am not one for following trends.

I grew up in the '70s and empowerment was not a concept applied to women back then. My dad was king. It was my mother's "job" to meet his every need.

What is happening? I said to myself.

My family was all seated at the dinner table when suddenly spoons, knives, and forks started flying around the room. Shocked, I looked in the direction of my father, who, as always, was seated at the head of the table. But he wasn't serving the dinner plates to each person as was his custom. Instead, his face was contorted with rage and he was throwing pieces of silverware in the direction of my mother. I froze. I heard a few more clanking sounds as the flying silverware struck parts of the dining room. Then, his rage spent, he stormed off to his bedroom, slamming the door behind him.

"Let's eat," my mother said cheerfully, without batting an eye. "The food is getting cold."

My mother didn't smile much, but she had a smile plastered on her face as she said this. She then went around to the head of the table and began serving the plates to me, my brother, and my sister. We ate our dinner in silence. Fortunately, my father hadn't hit anyone. My father never emerged from his room that night. He was already at work when we left for school the next morning, and by the time we sat down to dinner everything was back to normal. The incident was never ever discussed; in fact, to this day I have absolutely no idea what he was angry about.

My mother had done her job that night. As I look back, I realize that she was only able to express herself outside the home, through her community activities with other women. I understand that she was a force to be reckoned with in that arena.

Things have obviously changed since the 1970s. There are many more women in the workplace. They are earning higher salaries and hold leadership positions now. That is wonderful, but it doesn't necessarily mean that women are feeling or becoming more empowered. Becoming empowered is about how we feel internally about ourselves. Outward accomplishments can help us to become empowered, but we can have many accomplishments and still not be or feel empowered.

"I have been accepted to law school," I shouted into the phone.

My father's response: "You should stay home with your children."

Fortunately, I didn't do as my father ordered. He showed his displeasure to me for some time.

Once I became a lawyer, I took the first job offered to me because I had three children to support. I didn't put any thought into "my career." Women, especially women who were mothers, didn't really think they had much bargaining power or options. On job interviews, the interviewer (always a male partner at the law firm) would ask me what my husband did for a living and what I did with my children when I came to work, especially if they were sick.

"You can't ask those questions," my eldest daughter told me when she was applying for her first job. I laughed and replied, "Tell them that."

Chapter 12
Becoming Empowered

A few years later I got divorced, in part because my husband couldn't handle that I was better educated and earned more money than he did. I tried so hard to salvage the marriage by playing down my accomplishments. It worked for a while, but eventually I got tired of doing it and he was so full of rage it couldn't be contained no matter what I said.

"You are a single mother now!" the partner exclaimed. "I would never have hired you if I knew you would get divorced." If I complained about anything, he would respond, "You should just be happy we will let you keep your job." I rarely complained, even when I found out that I was paid less and did more work than the male associates. "No one else will hire you," the partner opined. And sadly, he was right.

I was a litigation attorney in a field where there were very few women. "You are a bitch," the other lawyer said to me. At first, I wanted to cry and I tried to appease him. *If I am nice, he will stop bullying me,* I said to myself. I was delusional. The nicer I was, the more the other attorneys and even the judges dismissed and bullied me.

I was excluded in more subtle ways too. All the male lawyers would chat together during a break in the deposition proceedings but I was not included. It was a way of making me feel small.

This was a blessing because it started me on my journey of becoming empowered. I began to stop trying to please and appease others—employers, judges, attorneys, and clients. Part of it was simply because I didn't have the energy to do that any longer while working long hours with three small children at home. The other part was how good it felt to stand up to them. The first time I did that was when I finally got so angry it just spilled out. I was shaking inside and totally doubting myself. It felt good to say what I wanted to say, to be who I wanted to be, and to do what I thought was right. This was the first step on my journey to becoming empowered. For a long time, it was "fake it 'til you make it."

Eventually I earned the respect of the other lawyers, which I have found is much better than being "liked." I was included in the chats during deposition breaks. We need to accept that we are not going to be liked by everyone. We need to remove that as one of our values or validations in life because it holds us back from becoming empowered.

I learned to validate myself rather than looking to be validated by others. I started asking myself, *Is what I'm thinking the right thing for me?* instead of how I could do what others were expecting me to do. After being conditioned to suppress my needs and desires it took some real time and effort to discover what I wanted and who I was. I'm still doing that, though it has gotten much easier with practice.

I also used to judge and criticize myself about everything. I learned to stop doing that—most of the time anyway. I stopped the negative talk about myself. I was told that the negative self-talk was character-building—critiquing and criticizing all the mistakes I had made in a day. It's not. It is just a way to keep me feeling like I am a bad person and to keep me from feeling empowered.

My Lessons of Empowerment
- I learned to validate myself rather than looking for validation from others.
- I spent time discovering who I wanted to be.
- I spent time discovering what I wanted in my life.
- I stopped judging and criticizing myself.
- I learned to forgive myself.
- I gave myself positive and uplifting messages.

What I do to be Empowered

When I am feeling empowered, I am feeling powerful because I am saying things to myself that are positive and uplifting. I am

Chapter 12
Becoming Empowered

feeling powerful because I am taking action that is aligned with how I feel, what I value, and who I want to be. I am being authentically me. I don't feel like an imposter. I am making decisions that will shape my life the way I want it to be. That is not to say that I never make mistakes and do things I regret. However, I don't berate myself now. I recognize the mistake. I try to correct it, especially if I have wronged someone else. Then I forgive myself. I am showing love for myself. Some people call it self-compassion.

Empowerment is different for every woman. It is learning what it is that you really want to be and what you want to do. It is not about imposing our will on others as has been done to us. It is about giving yourself permission to be and do what you want to do even if it disappoints and pisses some people off. Becoming empowered takes some courage.

If I abdicate to the needs of the other important persons in my life it is a conscious choice that I make. It comes from a place of strength, not weakness like before. Since it is a conscious choice, I am not resentful when I do it. I do it freely and happily. I am confident enough that if I abdicate to another at times, I will not lose myself.

"The handling of this matter has been totally wrong," the speaker at the meeting said. "We need to pivot and adopt a totally different strategy. We need to remove Craig from the case because he isn't doing a good job." *Well, I can listen to him and then just go do what I think is right,* I thought to myself, but that made me feel small and dishonest. Suddenly I said, "I disagree. I think Craig is being singled out unfairly and I don't think our entire strategy is wrong." (I won't bore you with all the details.) I wasn't as disrespectful or angry as I would have been in the past when expressing myself. The leader of the meeting was a bit shocked and not particularly happy with me, but afterward several people who were at the meeting came up to me and said they agreed with what I said and were glad I had spoken up. Standing up for what I thought was right felt so good and empowering. I could also look my colleague, Craig, in the eye when I saw him.

Community and Empowerment

We have, in my opinion, become too focused on being independent. Being independent is a big part of becoming empowered but it is also about community. We are empowered when we connect with our authentic selves—the independent part. We are even more empowered when we connect with others—our community. Connecting to community supports us and when we feel supported, we can be more authentic. When we act from a place of authenticity we are empowered.

The fastest and easiest way to connect with ourselves and others is through compassion. Self-compassion means being kind to ourselves, especially in difficult times. Instead of criticizing and judging ourselves we offer ourselves support and kindness. The same is true for others. When we see others struggling we offer them kindness and support, rather than judging and criticizing them.

When I stopped judging and criticizing myself, I was able to stop judging and criticizing others. I was more forgiving of others. I stopped seeking "perfection" and a feeling of superiority. I started to acknowledge my humanity and the humanity of others.

Once I stopped judging others, I stopped worrying that they were judging me. I felt more freedom to be who I wanted to be because I wasn't automatically assuming others were judging and criticizing me for who I was and what I did. It was liberating and empowering. That is not to say that I am naïve enough to think that others are not still judging and criticizing me. It just doesn't matter anymore.

I still have days when…! Life never moves in a straight line. But most days I wake up with a happiness that I am who I want to be and that is reflected in the choices I make and the life I am living. I am empowered.

Chapter 12
Becoming Empowered

ABOUT THE AUTHOR: Virginia Sampson is an attorney, writer, and speaker committed to helping others find their voice and power. Virginia would describe her childhood self as timid, frightened, and anxious. As an adult, she faced several challenges, from domestic violence and divorce to becoming a stepmother, full-time caregiver to her second husband, widowhood, and single motherhood. In working through these and other experiences Virginia was able to drop limiting beliefs, find her voice, and live authentically. She is passionate about helping others to do the same through her books, speaking, and programs where she provides the building blocks to assist others with their journey.

Virginia Hunter Sampson
virginiahuntersampson.com
virginiahuntersampson@gmail.com
512-980-4610

CHAPTER 13

Nurture Your Soul and Start Living Whole

Sarah Hauth

The first time a piece of my soul was chipped away, I was just three years old. My parents and I were living in Portland, Oregon, in a house owned by one of my dad's relatives. The house had been purchased back when the surrounding area was still rather rural farmland; however, at the time we lived there it had become, as my parents referred to it, the "White Ghetto." One morning—and I remember this vividly as if it was yesterday—there was commotion coming from the house directly across the street. Cop cars, their sirens blaring, raced into the driveway with an ambulance not far behind, and all sorts of people were streaming in and out of the home. The two men who lived there were brothers and junkies; one of them had a thirteen-year-old son I saw coming and going from time to time. Now that boy was emerging from the home, only this time he was zipped up in a body bag. I remember seeing two medics carrying the bag out and just knowing it was the boy. I could also feel evil energy permeating the air. I remember feeling frightened, sick, scared, confused, and a whole host of other emotions I had yet to feel in my small body. Looking back, I would pinpoint this as the moment

I began to feel I could not trust adults; it's also when I began to step away from myself.

At age five, right about time I started kindergarten, my parents moved us out of the "White Ghetto" to their slice of heaven: a forty-acre property on the coastal foothills, just six minutes from the beach near Pacific City on the Oregon coast. Although we had no visible neighbors, there was a farm "next door" with a single-wide trailer house on the other side of the pasture from us. The family had three kids: the oldest girl was one grade above me, the boy was in my class, and their younger sister was two grades below me. I loved playing with them. Between our property and their one-hundred-plus acres, we had a whole homestead and then some to ourselves. We were a pack of hooligans, spending the days outside, building forts, and exploring the forest, and generally running amuck. Our fun didn't end at the end of the day either—both properties bordered timberlands that had not yet been clear cut, and we'd often leave at dusk to roam around and only return when hunger demanded it.

They had an uncle who often babysat them. One day, I called to see if I could come play. The oldest sister answered and said, "Yes, come over." I ran over the hill, as I had done so many times before, but this time when I opened the door, I noticed she looked paler than usual. She was fair-skinned and a redhead so she was already pale, but that day she was as white as a ghost. She was sitting in the hall next to the door, hugging her knees tightly to her chest. When I asked her what was wrong, all she said was her sister's name. I looked up and watched as her uncle carried her sister into the kids' room. The girl's eyes met mine and though I registered the fear on her face I didn't realize what was happening. But, just as when the boy across the street had died back in Portland, I could feel a looming, haunting darkness, as well as extreme anxiety, fear, and confusion.

Until recently, I had more or less blocked most of this memory (it

Chapter 13
Nurture Your Soul and Start Living Whole

would be retrieved during my soul retrieval and a past life therapy session). While it didn't feel as though I was sexually mistreated that day, I do have an earlier recollection of being at the trailer with my friends and their uncle watching us. I don't recall any physical abuse that day either, but I am not completely certain as the memory is fuzzy. I do remember my mom asking me if I was raped, but I was scared and most likely didn't even know what rape meant at that age. All I know is that after this event, I felt a guilt for my life. Guilt that my parents needed to work to feed me and take care of me. Now, they are the most loving parents a girl could ask for and NEVER gave me this indication, only unwavering love and support. Yet the dis-ease, guilt, and that feeling that I was a burden persisted.

There were other memories from childhood that I only began to understand decades later. I recall one day, when I was around age twelve, feeling really upset. I was doing a terrible job at the time of expressing myself and, looking back, I don't think I even understood what I was so frustrated about. It is only in hindsight that I understand the reason. My parents had been in a years-long legal fight with the neighbors after they decided to clear cut several acres of trees along the property line. In doing so, they also cut a good swath of timber from my parents' side, sold the trees as their own, and never intended to come clean with my folks about the discrepancy. To make matters worse, the price of timber was at a premium at the time. My parents were hardworking and of modest means, but they put up the money and hired a law firm to represent them for the trespass of timber harvest. Since this had been going on for several years, I felt they were being bullied. I took on emotions and energy for something that was not my fault, out of my control, and didn't understand. I was pissed!

During my high school days, a plethora of dominoes fell in such a way that left my delicate developing body in fight-or-flight, from battling mononucleosis and teenage love triangles to the trauma of seeing my parents getting busted for growing pot in the late '90s. All of these conditions, some that were in my control and some that were not, were taking their toll on my body. I spent my twenties battling concurrent vaginal yeast and bacterial infections, so frequent that I was called, lovingly, by my closest friends and family as "Hot Box Betty." Unknowingly, my birth control pills, high-sugar diet, alcohol consumption, and emotional stress were contributing to this condition and setting the stage for the next health collapse that would occur in my late thirties.

One day, while playing with my six-year-old son, I noticed I couldn't even run thirty feet without becoming so winded I needed to stop and sit down. Suddenly, I was disgusted with myself. I was fat, tired, and physically so unkempt that I couldn't even enjoy a fun moment with my son. As I sat feeling like a beached whale on my couch, struggling to untie my shoes, I knew it was time to get the baby weight off. The very next day I was back at my gym and scheduled a nutritional meeting with my coach. In about three months of eating on plan and hitting two to four classes a week, I had not only shed the extra pounds but was in the best physical condition of my life. I looked good, felt good, and felt very accomplished for my hard work. However, my body was about to send me a major wake-up call to let me know I was not done learning her lessons.

It was as if someone flicked a switch. On October 31, I was in tip-top shape, and on November 1, I felt like my organs had been pushed through a meat grinder. For the next five months, I was bedridden. In the years preceding this seemingly sudden collapse of my health, I had been a terrible listener when it came to the messages my beautiful body was sending me. I ignored her wishes, wisdom, and truest heart's desires. In doing so, I grew an internal darkness. I believed I needed to fix something, everything, everyone; do more; strive for bigger achievements, and prove I could do whatever it was. Meanwhile, I ignored all the pieces that

Chapter 13
Nurture Your Soul and Start Living Whole

make me *me,* because it was just too painful to come clean with myself. Coming clean would mean I would hurt people I loved, and become a disappointment. Failing or not being the best at everything, and, God forbid, disappointing people in my life, was simply not an option. So instead, I hid my feelings. I stuffed them so deep into my gut that they literally pushed their way out of my body in the angry rage that is rectal prolapse. The all-consuming fight-or-flight frequency I had been marinating in for years had finally caught up to me.

My medical doctor told me, "There is nothing I can do for you. You have the digestive system of a ninety-year-old. Here are some suppositories and a tube of lidocaine. Good luck." I was devastated, yet something in my heart and soul told me there is another way. As I lay in bed, contemplating how I got there, I chose to learn every day how I could improve my physical condition. This time, likely because I was so desperate to get out of the physical pain I was in, I began to listen to my inner voice. I devoted months of reading into acupuncture theory, Chinese medicine philosophy, and how to eat to support digestion. I learned our organ systems have seasons when they are stronger and weaker. I realized I am just like a delicate hothouse flower. Summer is my strong season. Fall into winter is my weakest season. Soon I was led down a Taoist rabbit hole and shown the link between our thoughts and how the body becomes the mind—essentially, that our emotions are connected to physical health and well-being. My mind exploded with all this new information. Although still in my physical misery, I was connecting more deeply with a thousand-year philosophy than anything I had ever read. I became super-excited, especially when I discovered the work of Dr. Joe Dispenza and Dr. Bruce Lipton.

A few years later, I crossed paths with a friend who told me about this incredible medical device, called an Electro-Equiscope, she had purchased. The next day I called to schedule some sessions with her. As I learned more, I realized the Electro-Equiscope was going to be my ticket to regaining my quality of life. Basically, it's acupuncture on steroids. Three sessions in, I was by no means healed, but I could feel things getting stirred up in my body. With my friend's encouragement, I attended a training and returned completely lit up about this device and its healing potential. I knew then that in addition to healing myself I had to share it with others.

Within a month of owning my own Equiscope, I had myself more or less physically healed up. However, the emotional torment still festered inside of me. I still wasn't aware of or honoring the mind-body-spirit connection. It wasn't until life imploded further that I sought out spiritual work.

My soul retrieval was the single most profound experience of my life. Ten ages were called to my immediate awareness, and for each I could identify major life events, tragedies, emotional conflicts, matters of the heart, and loss. These events had triggered patterns of behavior that followed me throughout my life, affecting my physical and mental health in grossly negative ways. I wasn't even aware that this was the source of my misery until this beautiful ceremony was practiced upon me.

At four in the morning following the energetic soul retrieval part of the ceremony, I had a very lucid experience, which was very interesting as I've had very few dreams I can remember. In fact, years would pass between these dreams. In this one, I was in the backyard of my parents' house. It was at night. The back porch light was turned on, and I could see the coastal dew making each blade of vibrant green grass sparkle and shine brightly. I looked up toward the sky, and as I did a being floated down through the air. This being was shimmering in pure energetic vibration and dressed as Alice in *Through the Looking Glass,* but it was me. It was my face, my blonde hair pulled up into a ponytail with bangs combed forward. I somehow knew I was supposed to lie down into her. And

Chapter 13
Nurture Your Soul and Start Living Whole

as I did, I woke up. I sat up crying, hot tears streaming down my face, and said aloud, "Welcome home. I am home."

ABOUT THE AUTHOR: Sarah Hauth is a writer, mother, entrepreneur, and founder of the mobile health and wellness company, Simply Electric Life. She graduated from Linfield College with a Bachelor of Science in Management. Her past entrepreneurial ventures include Ego Drum Supply, a custom musical drum business, and Smith Rock Cannabis Company, an OLCC-licensed recreational marijuana producer. Sarah's health transformation journey utilizing Electro-Equiscope and spiritual integration have led her to her current path of sharing her story and inspiring others to take control of their own physical and spiritual healing.

Sarah Hauth
Simply Electric Life
Simplyelectric.life
Sarah@simplyelectric.life
541-364-1160

CHAPTER 14
A Message from Green Tara
Kathy Sipple

Many of us dream of a better, safer, more caring world, without recognizing that it all begins with creating and maintaining a deeper love in our own home. The seeds of world peace should be planted in our own backyard.
~ Anthon St. Maarten, Divine Living: The Essential Guide to Your True Destiny

Spread Too Thin

It's a cold December day in Valparaiso, Indiana, yet I am warm beneath wonderful-smelling soft blankets on the massage table. "What brings you here?" my new massage therapist asks. I share the details of my recent car accident. A driver ran a red light and t-boned my SUV, leaving it totaled and me with a mess of paperwork as well as some pinched nerves, restricted neck movement, and pain. The silver lining: I finally replaced the destroyed vehicle with a used Prius—an eco-friendly move I had been wanting to make for several years.

Before the chaos of the accident settles, I lose my primary source of income as a corporate social media marketing trainer when the company that hires me files for bankruptcy. I enjoyed the work a lot at the beginning. Besides it paying well, it was a thrill going to distant cities and working in beautiful meeting rooms with interesting people. But keeping up with the demands of travel and all the changes in technology had become exhausting and I had begun to yearn for a simpler existence. A few full-time positions come up and parts of them sound good, but they're not fully me. A distant memory resurfaces—I remember telling my husband years ago that I wanted to change my career focus in 2020—20/20, a new vision, a new me! I had been half-joking then, when 2020 seemed so very far away. Now 2020 is upon me and I don't feel ready. I don't know what's next but I know I need to hold out for work that makes me feel fully alive.

I love my part-time job as a Regional Resilience Coordinator with Earth Charter Indiana, but the one-year contracted position will be up in June. Reliant on grant-funding, their budget only allows for twenty hours monthly from me. Climate resilience is a huge job—much more than one person can handle in five hours a week! Luckily, I have met an incredible team of volunteers and together we host a Climate Action Blitz in February. It is very successful, attracting citizens from thirteen communities in Northwest Indiana and featuring lots of great speakers and presentations. Many new connections are made and vows taken, committing to contact local elected officials to encourage passing climate resolutions in their towns or cities. The success is bittersweet, though, for I know I need to find another job and will likely not be able to afford as much time working on environmental issues.

Green Tara's Message

I land an administrative part-time job to supplement my environmental work. I am not excited about it but rationalize that a bird in the hand is worth two in the bush. It's not in alignment with my skills or values, but it's only temporary. Since it doesn't begin until mid-March I decide to roadtrip to Cincinnati to visit my family. I sense my parents are worried about me; they sense I am not my usual enthusiastic self.

My mother is a gifted reiki healer; she offers me a treatment and

Chapter 14
A Message from Green Tara

I gladly accept. During my session I "see" a woman I recognize as the High Priestess from my tarot deck. She invites me to follow her behind a veil that covers the opening of her sacred temple. She guides me past other manifestations of the Divine Feminine until we arrive before a graceful, serene woman who I only vaguely recognize. "Are you Tara?" I ask her. "I am Green Tara," she answers. "Earth needs you at this time for its healing. You must heal yourself as well. You must regain your sovereignty, free yourself to do the work that is needed. Time is of the essence. Do not be afraid."

I know very little about Green Tara prior to her "visit," but I quickly do some research online and am grateful for this meaningful experience. I excitedly share the message from Green Tara around the dinner table with family that night. A phone call from my worried husband disturbs the reverie. He tells me the first case of COVID-19 in Indiana has been reported and the governor is declaring a public health emergency. The next morning I drive home anxiously, without stopping.

Getting My House in Order

Kindness, respect, compassion, and encouragement are the compost tea of relationships—they feed all the beneficial impulses. When we respect one another's ideas, think well of one another's motives, and support one another's visions, we create a high-energy atmosphere in which creativity flourishes.
~ Starhawk

As March unfolds my calendar clears—the job I was to begin is on hold due to the pandemic. Likewise, a paid out-of-town speaking engagement and even the local Earth Day celebration I was supposed to emcee are canceled! No more massage or travel for a while... My life plans, along with the lives of many, are suspended indefinitely.

I connect with friends near and far via Zoom. My ego still wants me to plug into "big" things of international importance, to be the heroine who leaves her mark on the world and offers comfort in this time of adversity. The first few days I am glued to my screen, offering a listening ear to others who are struggling with the challenges of coronavirus and how to adapt.

I develop a headache that doesn't go away for weeks. Each time I try to return to online meetings my body rebels. I hear Green Tara's voice and she is telling me to go outside.

The weather is warming. I decide this unexpected downtime is the perfect opportunity to convert our front yard from a traditional lawn to native plants and raised bed gardens for flowers and food. If I do this, it will definitely be an outlier in my neighborhood of traditional-looking lawns so I seek input from neighbors via our Facebook group, sharing a rendering of my vision and some of my reasons for wanting to do it: reduce or eliminate the need for mowing, allow for some food production, improve drainage for our yard and the surrounding area, and provide better habitat for pollinators. I am grateful and a bit surprised that no one objects—comments are neutral to positive. I proceed with sheet mulching, an ancient technique for converting grass to garden beds in preparation for the micro prairie I will install to replace our existing lawn.

Garden centers are closed due to the pandemic so I get creative about sourcing the materials I need. On trash pickup day I get up early to appropriate cardboard boxes my neighbors leave on the curb. Other friends offer me plant starts. I offer them homemade pizza and bread in return. The yard looks a mess as construction is underway but I have a beautiful vision and I see it taking shape. My body's flexibility is restored and I notice I am no longer in pain, just the regular muscle soreness from digging, bending, and lifting. I feel stronger and leaner. I sleep well at night.

By the end of May my native plants and heirloom vegetables are all planted. I'm already noticing more diverse wildlife. I spot a bird I've never seen before—a Northern Flicker—in my yard. I also notice more hummingbirds than ever, along with lots of dragonflies, butterflies, and toads too. All of this new life at home

Chapter 14
A Message from Green Tara

in my yard brings me joy.

Social Climate

For centuries seekers have been looking for a holy place on Earth. They believe it is called Shambala and that in that place a connection can happen between anyone and the universal wisdom. ...And they will not find it if they keep searching this way, for Shambala is inside each of us, and its outward manifestation is recreated by people. ~ Anastasia via Vladimir Megre, The Dimension of Love

By July I'm enjoying the fruits of my labors—I sit outside in the shade of my trellised vining plants and read a book, occasionally waving hello to neighbors as they pass by. I offer a pepper to a young dad walking by with his two young boys in a stroller. Another neighbor brings me some of her homemade baklava and I give her some yellow squash as a thank you. Another neighbor tells me seeing our yard makes her happy every time she passes it; our conversation about the environment deepens and she asks me for resources so she can explore further. I am grateful my yard has become a space that connects me not only to wildlife and the Earth but also more to my neighbors, especially in a time that otherwise feels very socially isolating.

With the yard transformation complete and the temperatures getting too hot for intense outdoor labor, I yearn to return to purposeful, fulfilling work. Right on cue, my Executive Director at Earth Charter Indiana tells me they have secured funding that will enable me to continue for another year and to expand my role as well.

Buoyed by the show of support, I deepen my commitment to the environmental work with a team of incredibly intelligent, passionate volunteers. We meet weekly online and I find I never have headaches with this group and this work. I take it as my body's feedback that I am on the right path.

We name ourselves Northwest Indiana (NWI) Region Resilience.

We create a logo, a website, and a social media presence. We decide on a shared aim—to facilitate a region-wide greenhouse gas emissions inventory to determine a baseline we can improve upon through future climate action plans. It is a long process to get buy-in from local elected officials and the regional planning commission, but we succeed! With help from Indiana University's Environmental Resilience Institute and six climate fellows, we complete Indiana's first-ever regional greenhouse inventory. The next year we complete a regional climate action plan framework, another first for the state.

The work keeps pulling me in, stretching me to do more, to think more creatively in order to achieve more in a short time. A new client engages me for my marketing services but I end up learning about sociocracy, a form of dynamic governance, from them. I realize learning this skill is just what I need to guide the complex process required for our climate work.

All the while, my beloved garden nurtures me. It is a place of both sanctuary as well as connection with friends and neighbors during the pandemic when meeting outdoors was considered safer and easier. My garden catches the attention of a local magazine editor who features photos of it along with a story about how native plants help not only wildlife but also are a beautiful, nature-based climate solution since they sequester carbon, help regulate stormwater drainage, and even clean water too. The local garden club sees the article and asks to include my garden on their annual garden tour. Nearly three hundred people tour my yard and their surveys say mine was the favorite. They are intrigued by what is possible in a small space and some seem willing to rethink their lawns in favor of creating wildlife habitats instead.

The work is not complete—within me, my garden, or our climate work. All of it will always be work in progress, I realize. It's 2023 and NWI Region Resilience has decided that in order to engage more people in nature-based climate solutions we will become the

Chapter 14
A Message from Green Tara

first-ever regional wildlife habitat certified by the National Wildlife Federation. We launch during April and quickly achieve most of the requirements with the rest well within reach through the cooperative efforts of a dynamic and dedicated team of supporters.

What else is possible if we learn to work together more harmoniously, I wonder. For today, I am grateful for the butterflies drawing sustenance from flowers I have planted. I'm grateful to wave to neighbors that were once acquaintances and now considered friends. I'm grateful for the gift I have been given through the work I am doing and our team's success. I am grateful for my garden's bounty. I am grateful that I listened to the message from Green Tara, who urged me to pursue my dreams and reclaim my sovereignty.

ABOUT THE AUTHOR: Kathy Sipple is available to help communities build resilience through Asset-Based Community Development, permaculture, and the facilitation of consent decision-making. She is working on a book, Healing Earth Together, expected to be published in 2024. The book will serve as a guide for communities to address environmental and social justice issues while enriching their own quality of life. Sipple holds a degree in Economics from the University of Michigan and is a member of Mensa. She lives in Valparaiso, Indiana with her husband John. She enjoys frequent hikes at the Indiana Dunes.

Kathy Sipple
CoThrive Community
kathysipple.com
kathy@kathysipple.com
219-405-9482

CHAPTER 15

True Love

Heather Dare

One hot summer day, my life changed forever. I was at home with my two small children, my boxer, Max, and a former co-worker's one-and-a-half-year-old daughter, who I was babysitting. I had been a stay-at-home mom for the past two and a half years, ever since getting laid off from my job as Director of Recruiting for an Anesthesia Practice. It couldn't have come at a more perfect time. They had given me the option to stay with a pay cut; however, I was eight months pregnant with my first child, and while the company did not offer paid maternity leave, they did offer a generous severance package. It was a no-brainer.

Like most mothers of young children, I was exhausted. My youngest was just seven months old and still getting up at night; my days were spent caring for him and chasing the toddlers around. The only time I had to myself was in the morning before my husband left for work, and I used that time to go running. I had always exercised, even during my pregnancies, because I knew how important and healthy it was. Yet, my morning runs were full of panic and anxiety. It's when my feelings of not being able to handle caring for the children anymore seemed to emerge. I remember telling my husband that I wanted to stop babysitting, that it had become too much for me, but he had financial concerns. I felt this financial pressure as well and wanted to contribute.

I felt like I couldn't relax or sit down. There was always something to be done. One of the kids always needed me to meet their needs for comfort, entertainment, or feedings. I was always cooking and cleaning. Worse than all of that, though, was the fear. I was afraid I was hurting the children no matter what I did. Memories from my own childhood—specifically the mental, physical, and emotional abuse I witnessed and experienced—began to creep into my mind. I remember brushing my kids' hair and feeling as though I was hurting them. When I bathed them, I felt like the water was never the right temperature or that I was being too rough. The fear of hurting them was so great that I started pacing, having panic attacks, and breaking out into a sweat. I wanted to treat them with love but felt like I didn't know how, based on how I had been treated. It got to the point where I was even nervous about being alone with them. I was living in a constant state of panic.

All of this came to a head on that summer day. I was outside on our back deck with the kids as they were playing. I was so angry. I was full of rage. I was sweating, pacing, and feeling as though I was going to hurt someone. Max barked at me and jumped on me as if he sensed my despair. Finally, I called my husband at work and told him he needed to come home. I called my former coworker and told her she needed to come get her daughter. When they arrived, I was crying. I felt like such a failure because I couldn't handle it. I needed help. I couldn't continue to live like this.

I called my OB/GYN's office. They were the last folks who had talked to me about postpartum depression and anxiety. I remember driving to their office, alone and scared. The doctor handed me a questionnaire that asked about my thoughts and feelings toward myself and I completed it. I was crying. I was shocked at my own answers and feelings. I was suicidal! The doctor's solution was to take medication for the depression and to see a mental health

Chapter 15
True Love

therapist. Though I was opposed to medication and feared addiction, I took it. I was that desperate to feel better.

That night I woke up at two a.m. I was hallucinating. I was seeing numbers running through my mind. I was scared and constantly worrying. I couldn't sleep. The days were just as bad. I was still having panic attacks. I was scared to be alone with my thoughts; I didn't even want to be alone to shower and shave for fear that I would self-harm. I didn't want to hurt myself or my boys. I called my mother to let her know what was going on, and she came to stay with us for a while to help out.

The following week I had my first appointment with a mental health counselor. I explained everything I had been going through, including the hallucinations. She said they were most likely a psychotic break from the medication and to come off it. She also said I had PTSD, anxiety, and major depression.

Once I was diagnosed, my symptoms worsened. It was as if I couldn't focus on anything else. Worry overtook me as I read about the impacts these conditions could have on my children. I started paying even more attention to the boys, making sure I was making eye contact and bonding with them. They deserved love from me and they deserved for me to be happy and healthy.

This was only the beginning of a very long journey of healing. I no longer had a sense of self and no self-esteem. I remember my therapist asking me what I liked about myself and I wasn't able to name one thing. Yet, I was determined to overcome this; I was willing to do anything and everything in my power to get better, to be a happy and healthy mom for my kids. I started cognitive behavioral therapy and worked on changing all of my thoughts about myself to positive ones. Every day, all day, I was changing my thoughts while caring for the children and playing with them, while cooking and cleaning. It was even more work than before.

A few weeks later, I did a Google search to find out what, other than talk therapy, helps with anxiety and depression. Yoga was at the top of the list, so I tried it at the gym. After that very first class, I felt more relaxed than I had in years. I kept attending classes and wanted to learn more about why yoga was helping me. Six months later, I enrolled in a yoga teacher training program. I had no intention of teaching, but I wanted to learn more. I wanted to heal. I wanted to learn about why I was depressed, anxious, and had PTSD.

During that first year of training, I changed my lifestyle completely. I incorporated my own yoga and meditation practice into each day, as well as the study of yogic philosophy daily. I changed my diet. I did less. I spent time on the weekends at yoga training. I created balance between caring for my sons and my personal development. I joined a local mothers' group, made new friends, and took the kids on playdates during the day. At night, I carved out time for my studies and yoga classes; I spent more time alone.

The combination of Cognitive Behavioral Therapy, mental health counseling, and yogic tools and techniques contributed to my healing and transformation. Physically, my body was more relaxed. I had less tension. I was more flexible. I lost a few pounds with the change in my diet, though I didn't have much weight to lose. I felt younger and lighter. Mentally, I had fewer thoughts, slower thoughts, and, sometimes, no thoughts! I was calmer and more peaceful. My sleep improved. I began to have more positive thoughts about myself organically, rather than having to work at changing negative thoughts. Also, I was no longer experiencing depression, panic, or anxiety on a regular basis. My emotions were more positive and I began to feel self-love for the very first time. I noticed I had more energy, and I was more loving and positive toward myself and others. I was sensitive to other people's energy too.

My spirituality also developed and evolved. I had been raised Catholic and went to Catholic school. I prayed every night before falling asleep. Over the years, however, my relationship with God

Chapter 15
True Love

had faded. Now, my connection with "The One" or "The Divine" grew stronger every day as I connected through prayer, yoga, and meditation. Once I rekindled that relationship, I really began to change.

One day, I was driving in the car with the kids and had this overwhelming nudge to do something with my hands. I took the boys to the craft store and looked around, my eyes landing on clay. I had no artistic background, yet the urge to make something was strong. I took the clay home and started playing with it and sculpting it. I had no idea what I was doing, yet somehow I was forming a sculpture of me and my sons! It was meditative and felt good. The sculpture turned out to be pretty amazing for a first-timer. I continued sculpting whenever I felt inspired and started painting and writing too. It was a true gift.

After that year of yoga training, I started teaching yoga and meditation in fitness centers, yoga studios, colleges, drug and alcohol rehabilitation centers, corporate centers, parks, and apartment complexes. I continued with Yoga Therapy training for three more years while I continued healing and growing. For the first time, I fully understood how the childhood abuse had impacted me and my self-worth and was able to let it go; I uncovered the causes of my anxiety and depression and was able to shift them as well.

During my last year of Yoga Therapy Training, I left my marriage. I realized I had married a man who treated me very similarly to the way my family treated me growing up. My husband and I fought for six months as I could no longer tolerate the put-downs and the lack of emotional connection. I wanted to be in a loving relationship. Our views on parenting were not in alignment either. When I asked him to go to counseling for his anger and he refused, I left with my boys and Max and moved in with my parents. It was the most difficult decision of my life.

It would also prove to be a very challenging time. My parents helped with the kids, but I needed emotional support they could not give me. They had been together since they were thirteen, and as Catholics they did not believe in divorce. In fact, they were very angry about my decision. This had been part of my belief system as well and I was experiencing a lot of guilt and shame. I soon found myself being parented by them again, as were my boys. I disagreed with their style of parenting because of the effects that it had on me. I had once again gone from one abusive environment to another.

    Eight months later, the kids and I moved out on our own. I worried about the boys and how they were handling all the changes. At night while lying in bed with them, I would talk about the divorce and why I left. I reassured them that it was not their fault and that they were so loved. Thankfully, they were incredibly resilient. After adjusting to life on my own, I decided to return to college for my bachelor's in psychology while I continued teaching yoga. I was so happy when I walked across the stage to get my degree, knowing my boys were in the audience.

    Then Covid happened. At the time, I co-owned a yoga studio where I was teaching classes in-person and online to amazing, supportive women. The physical studio closed at the tail-end of the pandemic because there were not enough folks attending classes in person. My business partner and I disagreed with the vision for the future of the studio, so we closed. I now have my own business online providing yoga classes, private yoga therapy sessions, and whole-person self-care programs for mothers and women with stress, anxiety, depression, and PTSD.

    Today, when I think back to that summer day when my life changed forever, I am filled with gratitude for my life, the healing, the transformation, and the self-love. Out of that darkness came the light. The darkness transformed into blessings and miracles that propelled me forward toward serving others, loving myself, and teaching my children how to love themselves so that we can

Chapter 15
True Love

spread that love to others. My darkness turned out to be the greatest gift of all…True Love.

ABOUT THE AUTHOR: Heather Dare is a Certified Yoga Therapist through the International Association of Yoga Therapists, a yoga and meditation educator, reiki practitioner, ordained minister, and clay sculptor. She discovered yoga during a challenging time in her life and found it to be instrumental in her physical, mental, emotional, and spiritual transformation. She especially resonated with Yoga Therapy—individual sessions involving the application of yogic principles, tools, postures, breath work, and meditation techniques within a therapeutic relationship. Today, Heather uses Yoga Therapy, along with other holistic health and wellness tools, to help and guide women with stress, anxiety, depression, and PTSD to a life of self-love and joy.

Heather Dare
heatherdareyoga.com
heatherdareyoga@gmail.com

CHAPTER 16

Beyond the Fear

Debbie Weiss

Can I tell you a secret? I'm almost afraid to commit it to the page, but here goes nothing…

My dream is to be an inspirational speaker. Not just a small-town speaker, but a speaker on big stages, arenas, concert venues, and stadiums. I want to impact as many people as humanly possible through the sharing of my story and my message.

Phew! I can't believe I just put that out there into the Universe. It's unfathomable to think that someone like me would be saying such a thing. You see, for most of my life, I have had no control of my own destiny.

Who did, you ask? A more appropriate question would be, *"What had the control?"*—and the answer is FEAR.

You might be familiar with this emotion too—and the sense that it was in the driver's seat of your life, making all the decisions. I allowed fear to rule the roost. I can remember being petrified of being seen as a little girl. I was chubby and always felt unworthy, ashamed, and insecure. I spent my life trying not to be noticed because I was afraid people would judge me.

So I'm sure you're wondering how anyone who lives their life in fear would want to stand up on big stages and be seen by everyone? Good question…it amazes me too!

Public speaking used to be on my top-ten list of things I was most afraid of, right behind sharks (at least after *Jaws* came out) and the monsters lurking in my closet. As a matter of fact, it stopped me for years from taking on a volunteer position I secretly dreamed of holding.

I had been very active in my Reform synagogue for many years—serving as treasurer for six years and vice president for three. Typically, the vice president went on to become president, however, I would only agree to take the VP job on the condition that I might choose not to assume this role. The last thing I wanted was to feel guilty about not doing what was expected of me.

So, why didn't I want to be president? There were a few reasons and all of them were ruled by my arch nemesis, FEAR.

1. *What if I did a bad job?*
2. *What if I couldn't effectively run a board meeting?*
3. *I would have to run our annual congregational meeting. What if I didn't know the answers to the questions congregants would ask? What if I had no idea what to say and said something stupid?*

The thing that terrified me the most, however, was the responsibility of addressing the congregation from the pulpit during the High Holy Days. It is the president's job on Rosh Hashanah and Yom Kippur (which are ten days apart) to give a speech during services asking the congregation for financial support. These two days have the highest attendance of the year, with approximately a hundred and fifty people in the synagogue (a hundred and forty-nine more than I was comfortable talking to at a time). That sealed the deal—I would never be president!

It was February 2018 when the call came in. The call I had been dreading. The call I had thought about over and over again in my mind. It was the call asking if I would become president when our new fiscal year began on July 1, 2018.

Based on the reasons above, my answer should have been an

Chapter 16
Beyond the Fear

emphatic "thanks, but no thanks." Instead, I simply said, "I would be honored."

Wait—*what*??? You read that right. I was as shocked as you are.

Two different thoughts had been on repeat in my mind for the months leading up to that call. The first was that my dad, who had always wanted to be president of our congregation, had a massive stroke a year before he was to take on that title. My dad passed away in 2011, and I felt by becoming president I would be fulfilling his dreams on his behalf. How could I say no?

The other loop playing in my head was that I was fifty-five years old and still allowing fear to control me. *If I declined, would I look back and regret it? Was I going to allow fear to take the reins yet again?* I had already been on a soul-searching, transformational journey for several years at that point, but I had yet to master my anxiety. Becoming president would be a brave, defiant step that would continue to move me in the right direction.

I was so excited and proud of myself when I uttered that yes! Of course, it was easy to say that in February, when my term didn't start for several more months. My presidency got off to a good start in July. I was finding my way and learning, as all new presidents do, and even feeling optimistic. *Maybe I can do this,* I thought to myself. The summer was relatively quiet at the temple so I had time to get my bearings. But the High Holy Days—and the speech I would have to give—were never far from my thoughts.

Writing the speech was the first hurdle. I didn't consider myself a writer and was concerned about being judged for not being smart enough. Many of my synagogue colleagues were the literary, intellectual, academic types and my style was more stream-of-consciousness writing. It was a reflection of how I think and speak, and I felt it wouldn't translate to a polished, eloquent, and captivating speech. I was sure the few people I allowed to review it beforehand thought it was juvenile and elementary, but I tried not to let their perceived opinions discourage me. In fact, I was quite pleased with how it turned out! It conveyed my message perfectly and was an open, honest representation of who I was. That meant toning down "the financial ask." I had to be me.

I practiced at home, trying to master the art of reading while occasionally looking up to make eye contact with the audience. The night before my big debut, I read it a few more times and was feeling pretty comfortable with it, so I put the pages down and went up to bed. You would have thought that I would be up all night worrying, but I wasn't. There was a lot of soothing self-talk going on in my head, and it actually soothed me to sleep!

And then I woke up...

The minute my eyes popped open the next morning, I could feel the internal trembling begin. *"Why the heck had I agreed to this? What possessed me to think I could do this? This was a horrific idea!"* Certainly not the best thoughts to begin the day.

I took a shower, did my makeup and hair with such precision that you'd think I was going to be examined and graded for the job I had done. I felt confident in how I looked and I read the speech once more before getting in my car to drive the few short miles to the temple. After chatting with the congregants, it was time to take our seats. Once the service began, I knew I had approximately eighty minutes until I had to take my place on the pulpit.

Just the idea of having all eyes on me as I took that walk from my seat in the audience was enough to make me sick. One hundred and fifty pairs of eyes watching my every move, looking at my clothes, hair, legs, et cetera... I thought I had repaired all those feelings of insecurity and unworthiness, but obviously I had not. As the service progressed, I started feeling seriously sick to my stomach. *What if I tossed my cookies right here in front of everyone? Maybe I should go to the bathroom and then text the rabbi and send him my apologies. I would tell him I was ill and had to leave. My speech*

Chapter 16
Beyond the Fear

was already on the podium, so he could read it for me.

I knew I would never do that, but it was nice to fantasize. Then, all of a sudden, it was time. He was introducing me.

Here goes nothing, I thought to myself.

It was quite a different perspective looking at the congregation from the pulpit, with all those eyes focused on me. My mouth was so dry the words seemed to get caught up in it. I then began to read, trying to contain the trembling in both my voice and my body. I was sure that it was insanely obvious just how totally frightened I was at that moment, but my only choice was to forge on.

The opening paragraphs contained a few sentences that were meant to be light and funny, and I happily looked up to see people smiling and chuckling. *Wow! They are listening. I am clearly doing okay.* The speech began with an explanation of why I had decided to become president. I didn't reveal the fear factor—that part wasn't ready for prime time just yet—though I did share that my dad's own journey in temple life had been one of the reasons I had accepted the role.

As I spoke of his passing years earlier, two very unexpected things happened. The first was that I choked up. All the times I had practiced the speech this had never happened. Being up on that pulpit, speaking to the congregation as its president, and thinking about my dad, brought up a surge of emotion. My eyes filled with tears and I paused, trying desperately to contain them.

The second unexpected thing that happened was I saw others with tears in their eyes. I had everyone's attention. No one was fidgeting or looking down at their lap, the floor, or their phone. They were engaged. They were hearing and feeling what I was saying. My words were impacting them. My regular person, no-frills words were touching them. I went from trembling to soaring with confidence and pride. I never wanted the feeling to end. *How had I lived for fifty-five years and never felt anything like this before?*

Once the service ended, there was a receiving line which I, as president, participated in. One person after another told me how my speech had touched them. They shared how my story made them think of their own stories. Some said it was the best speech (at least by our temple presidents) that they had ever heard. It was surreal listening to their praise and accolades. I was beaming and bursting with pride. I stood there in a dreamlike state, soaking in each and every moment.

The next day, while still basking in the afterglow, I realized I had to do this again in ten days. Part of me couldn't bear to wait that long to get back up there, while another piece of me once again felt fear. It wasn't the same fear as before, but rather the fear that I had set the bar too high. All these people were now expecting me to be moving and inspirational every time I spoke! Chances were good that I was a one-hit-wonder.

The speechwriting didn't flow for me as easily as it had the first time since I was now experiencing performance anxiety. After a few different starts and stops, I settled on a second product I was pleased with. My heart still raced during the service, waiting for the rabbi to introduce me, however, it wasn't beating quite as fast as it had been a week earlier. This time I had to ask a bit more directly for money, so it wasn't as emotional. I still received compliments while standing in line, but now they sounded a bit different. Initially, the comments were that of amazement. People had been surprised at my ability to convey a powerful, heartfelt message. This time the compliments were more matter of fact, like, "Wow! You're really good at this!'

I couldn't believe I had to wait an entire year to do it all again.

In just ten short days I had become a completely different person, and this transformation would never have happened if I had listened to my fearful inner voice. By facing my fear head-on, I opened up an entire world of possibilities for myself.

Chapter 16
Beyond the Fear

As I pursue my new goal of being a public speaker, I still feel afraid. Shame and unworthiness linger, but I know that beyond my fear lies a new life waiting for me. I'm ready to embrace this new life, even though it scares me.

ABOUT THE AUTHOR: With more than five decades of confronting life's most daunting challenges under her belt, Debbie Weiss is an expert in triumphing over limiting beliefs to achieve her dreams—and inspiring others to do the same. Debbie is the author of the memoir, On Second Thought, Maybe I Can, which is scheduled for publication in August 2023. A multifaceted entrepreneur, Debbie operates both an insurance agency and her online store, A Sprinkle of Hearts. She is also the host of the podcast Maybe I Can, as well as a speaker, a dedicated family caregiver, and a mother.

Debbie Weiss
debbierweiss.com
debbie@debbierweiss.com
908-892-0508

CHAPTER 17

Concussion: 0 | Heart: 1

How A Bang On The Head Led Me To My True Calling

Melissa Griffiths

There was nothing particularly unusual about the day that changed my life.

I woke up at the same time, I ate the same breakfast, I ran through the same frustrations in my head. I don't like to think of it as an accident; that implies it wasn't meant to happen. From all the healing work I have done since, I have learned that I was supposed to receive a head trauma on that not-very-unusual day.

By way of background, I'm a rather normal female living a rather normal life. Enough years under my belt to have "experience," yet not enough to be ignored at weddings. I am happily married with two boys who, at the time of my "accident," were ages four and two. I'm also a businesswoman, having spent my whole career working with accounting firms and law firms in a sales capacity.

Funny how careers happen. It seems one day you have dreams and expectations of being an astronaut, a vet, a supermodel, and the next you find yourself working with a bunch of gray-suited accountants and lawyers. Not that I have anything against accountants and lawyers—many remain my closest friends—it's just that it wasn't my first choice (or even on my radar) when I graduated university with a liberal arts degree.

Sales always sounded such like a dirty word—visions of greased back hair, flashing white teeth, and phrases such as "what will it take to get you into a car today" (a miracle) or "should we confirm for Tuesday or Thursday?" (neither). In fact, I did want to be a vet, but since I hated biology and couldn't stand to watch animals die, I had to adjust my expectations.

I never wanted children either. I was adamant that motherhood wasn't for me and truly, I meant it. It wasn't until I reached the age of forty and almost missed the proverbial boat, that I realized I did want to have kids after all. Imagine that! Thankfully, my husband and I got pregnant easily and had two boys in two years.

The "Accident"

And so it was that on the morning of September 3, 2016, I found myself standing in a muddy field watching a group of preschoolers play soccer. For anyone who has ever seen preschoolers play soccer, you will know that it isn't really "sport." It's a collection of toddlers running as a pack, trying desperately to kick the ball and missing frequently. Every now and then a foot will strike the ball and, since all the other kids are clustered behind it, it may or may not make it into the net. Proud parents analyze their kids' abilities and try to determine if a scholarship is in their future or if they should switch and pursue baseball instead.

On this particular day, the soccer scramble had just ended and I bent down to pick up my backpack. As I moved downwards, one of the kids running towards me, looking behind him like little kids do, ran straight into my forehead. "Sorry!" he giggled, as he ran off. It was so innocuous. Such a silly little accident, barely even noticed by my husband, who was standing right next to me.

It took me two years to recover.

When he ran into me, I felt the shock reverberate throughout my whole body. Everything went white, then black, then eerily quiet. My teeth seemed to dissociate from my jaw and the ringing in my ears was intense. I couldn't see, I couldn't feel, I couldn't understand. I knew I had been hit in the head by a young kid but

Chapter 17
Concussion: 0 | Heart: 1

I couldn't understand why I was reeling so much. I felt like I was about to vomit and I slumped to the ground as my legs gave way. Somehow, I made it home and went straight to bed with the most incredible headache.

"Wow, that kid had a hard head," I commented as I laughed it off that night. "Imagine that a little body could give me such a headache!" I laughed it off again and ignored how I was feeling because, after all, I was only hit by a four-year-old. The next day I was still feeling uncomfortable so I lay on the couch all day and thanked my husband for taking care of the kids.

"I'm just tired," I said.

The next day was Monday, so I went to work. I felt awful but it was only a little bump so I just needed to get through it and I would be fine. As soon as I turned on my computer, I felt it. The room started spinning, the intense pressure in my ears started again, and this time I couldn't hold back the nausea. I went straight to the emergency room and was diagnosed with a concussion.

"Give it a few days," they told me. A few days became "two weeks," which became "about a month," which eventually became "We don't know how long it will take." I had to go on disability leave as I could barely stand up. I took every possible test that Western medicine could give me—from CAT scans to MRIs, vision tests, hearing tests, Epley maneuvers. For the next six months I was poked and prodded by specialists at Stanford and the University College of San Francisco. Nothing. Nada. Zip. Nobody could figure out what was wrong with me and why I wasn't improving.

Eventually I had to go back to work as I just couldn't lie in bed any longer. While working was a momentous effort, it was better than being in bed with my dark, dark thoughts. I was a terrible parent—my kids made my head spin and I missed two years of their plays and school presentations. My work output was awful and I went from being the top performer for ten-plus years to barely selling anything. I didn't want to use my accident as an excuse—after all, it was only a four-year-old who hit me—yet I really struggled to do anything.

Depression was real and my self-confidence was through the floor. My husband was incredibly supportive but even he was losing patience with how hard simple tasks were. I went from being a high-functioning executive who used to run marathons in my spare time to not even being able to walk my kids the quarter mile to school. With that change came an incredible emotional burden.

I had lost hope in finding a solution. The doctors I worked with were fantastic but no one could do anything for me other than prescribe me more medication, which led to some horrible side effects. Desperate, I started researching concussions. It started out a pretty steep downward slope as I learned of people who had been suffering for more than twenty years with no end in sight. People who were suicidal and people who had sadly succeeded in ending their pain. It was dark and hard to read, and I knew I didn't want to go there. Through my research I came across something called "QHHT." After one session, my symptoms completely disappeared.

The Healing

QHHT (Quantum Healing Hypnosis Technique) is a form of hypnosis developed by Dolores Canon. She started in the 1960s using hypnosis to help people recover from physical symptoms, but as she conducted more and more sessions, something remarkable happened. She found that her patients were regressing into scenes from past lives. At first, she didn't believe it, but it happened more and more and then one day she connected with something even greater—what she called The Subconscious.

For Dolores, The Subconscious is a part of every person's mind that always exists just below the level of our conscious minds. Some people call it Source Energy, or Guides, or Guardian Angels. When contacted and communicated with, there is simply no question it cannot answer about an individual's current life, or about any of their past lives.

Chapter 17
Concussion: 0 | Heart: 1

I booked a session not really knowing what to expect. As the hypnosis progressed, I found myself on an island living in a stick house. My skin was black (in this life it is white) and I realized that I was severely disabled and unable to speak. I was in a type of wheelchair that had been built for me by the villagers, and while I could hear I couldn't speak or communicate. Surprisingly though, I wasn't frustrated. I was incredibly happy and content. I spent my days just "being" and found immense satisfaction in watching others play.

When we reached the part of the session where the practitioner asked my Subconscious why they had chosen to show me that life, the answer was that they wanted me to know I had been happy without perfect health and that happiness is a state of mind. The practitioner asked that now I had received this lesson, could my health be returned to me? The answer was yes.

In my drowsy state, I heard myself say "yes" and at that moment I started to spin. Not literally obviously, but every single cell of my body started to spin. I even felt the nails on my pinky toes spinning. They went clockwise, then counterclockwise, then clockwise again. I felt like I was a collection of individual cells and each of them was doing something independently, yet in perfect harmony. The whole process lasted about two minutes, which felt like an eternity. I couldn't move and yet every part of me was moving. The sensation was so intense I screamed for it to stop but it just got faster. Then just when I thought I was about to vomit, it stopped.

Silence. Stillness. Nothing. Like it never happened. The practitioner continued with the session. I have since learned that what I experienced was my body performing an upgrade. I needed to leave behind my old belief systems in order to live a new life. When I came out of the hypnosis, every single one of my concussion symptoms had gone completely. They have not returned.

Honestly, I wouldn't have believed it if it hadn't happened to me. It was so profound and life-changing that I wanted to learn more.

I devoured every piece of literature I could find on energy healing and learned that my story was not unusual—there were so many others who have come to realize that the body is capable of healing itself. Some of the stories were truly incredible and yet, true. It led to a rabbit hole for me.

The Shift

I qualified as a QHHT Practitioner as I felt drawn to helping others the way I had been helped. I took it further and pursued other modalities and in the space of a year I also qualified as a Certified BodyTalk Practitioner, a Certified Emotional Resolution Practitioner, and a Certified HeartMath® Practitioner. I learned everything I could about the brain and how it connects to the body, as well as how our body and our Subconscious talk to us through pain, emotions, and feelings.

During all this time I continued working in a corporate capacity. During the day I would don my business suit and run sales teams, then in the evenings and weekends I studied energy healing, listened to quantum physics podcasts, and researched recent developments in neuroscience. I didn't dare tell anyone what I was learning for fear of being classed as crazy, a bit weird, or, worse, spiritual.

I led two very different lives.

Working in corporate America became harder. I saw how stressed people were at work and then how they took that back to their homelives. From all my research, I had learned the importance that thoughts and emotions have on our health and it became harder to work in an environment that fed the stress, rather than helping it. I was connecting with extremely successful and wealthy people who were unhappy, miserable, anxious, and increasingly unhealthy as a result. I knew I needed to do something.

I declared to my long-suffering husband that I wanted to leave a very high-paying position and twenty-five years of sales experience to move into the healing business. Once again, he was incredibly supportive and we laid out a plan to get me there. The Universe had

Chapter 17
Concussion: 0 | Heart: 1

a shorter timeline, though, and a month before I was due to quit, my company made the decision to lay me off. I was astonished at how I had manifested such an outcome and while my heart goes out to everyone affected by layoffs, the feeling of relief and excitement was amazing.

The day after my layoff I set up my own healing business and haven't looked back. When you do something that is your purpose and passion, it doesn't feel like work. Every day I feel immense gratitude to the Universe for smacking me across the head and sending me down a healing path which was truly life changing. I look back at those two difficult years where I thought my life was over and realize that it was essential to making me who I am today. I am now convinced that things really do happen for a reason and it is how we choose to approach them that fuels our personal growth.

ABOUT THE AUTHOR: Melissa Griffiths is a Certified HeartMath® Mentor, Emotional Resolution Practitioner, BodyTalk Practitioner, Level 2 Quantum Healing Hypnosis Therapy Practitioner, and a Certified Clinical Anxiety Treatment Professional. For over twenty-five years Melissa lived by the hormones of stress as a business development executive, running national sales teams, working with Fortune 50 companies, and closing multi-million-dollar deals. In 2016, a freak accident left her with a severe concussion, adrenal fatigue, migraines, and depression. During her two-year healing process, she realized that her true value was teaching others how their thoughts, feelings, and emotions affect their physical body and overall health. Melissa founded Ascension, Inc. to share the tools and techniques that worked for her.

Melissa Griffiths
Active Ascension, Inc.
active-ascension.com
melissa@active-ascension.com

CHAPTER 18

My Healing Journey
The Path to My Spiritual Life Purpose
Pamela Emmert

The memories and specific life experiences of my early childhood remain mostly invisible and unknown to me. In recent years, my older sister has spoken of unpleasant events that happened in our younger lives. "Where was I?" I would ask in shock and confusion, for I had no such recollection. Her reply was always the same: "You were there, Pam. Don't you remember?"

What I Do Know

I do remember that my childhood was not joyful. My parents had a volatile and unhealthy relationship, which led to a vindictive divorce and an agonizing custody battle. I experienced years of separation from my mother and siblings. The cruel control and unthinkable actions of my father negatively impacted our lives. To this day, we each have repercussions from the shared and individual traumatic experiences because of the destructive dysfunctional circumstances within our family.

Mama Trauma

I do not remember how old I was when I first heard about what happened to me. The fact that I fell out of a two-story house window at just two years old was an interesting but startling story. This story was repeated over and over again with various versions, opinions, and details of how and why, and, more importantly, who was responsible for it.

Soon, *I* was the person who started bringing it up, especially during heated conversations with my mother about my childhood. She was the one who was supposed to protect me, so why did she abandon me? Wasn't she responsible for what happened to me? Why wasn't she a better mother?

I remember the look on my mother's face after one intense conversation in May 2016. It revealed for the first time, the guilt, regret, pain, and suffering that she felt as she solemnly said, "How long are you going to continue bringing up what happened that day?" In that moment, her words were like a dagger to the heart. I recognized that what had happened to me all those years ago also traumatized her. Ultimately I realized how much I was hurting her and vowed never to speak of it again.

As I write these words, I am still processing the recent loss of my mother. I dedicate this chapter to her memory and those who came before her and also endured a lifetime of traumatic experiences, as well as the next generation who have borne the weight of energetic cycles of abuse that carried forward. I am at peace with my own healing, hoping that the cycle of generational traumas suffered by the women in my family lineage stops with me and will not affect my children and grandchildren.

Daddy Trauma

The most painful years of my childhood were those when I felt nonexistent and insignificant to my father. While living with him, he provided basic food and shelter to me and my siblings, but the reality was he completely abandoned us. He was never home, which left me no choice but to care for my younger siblings. He chose life with a new girlfriend over the care of his children and the responsibilities as a parent.

I remember playing outside and watching his car approach our home after work, only to pass by and continue onto hers without so much as a wave or a honk. While I felt an innate responsibility

Chapter 18
My Healing Journey

to nurture and care for my siblings, the expectation to meet their physical and emotional needs, along with my own, was beyond the capacity of a thirteen-year-old.

For many years I struggled to face how helpless I felt to protect my family from the trauma they experienced. I worried about what would become of their lives. The damage was deeply rooted in all of us. I learned to bury and hide my own trauma and feelings of guilt, unworthiness, abandonment, and isolation as I attempted to find forgiveness, love, and acceptance. I eventually found the grace to forgive myself and others, and the will and inner strength to overcome and heal.

During the passing of my paternal grandmother, I gathered with my siblings and father. It was the first time he had seen some of his children in twenty-five to thirty years. I witnessed his repentance as he cried and acknowledged the horrible things he had done in his life, testifying that his mother would be ashamed of him.

Four years later, my siblings and I gathered again around our father as his frail body was preparing to transition to the Spirit world. There was significance in the fact that we all came; it was a fated healing opportunity. We comforted him, each other, and ourselves. I was able to spend time caring for him, and as the end approached I found peace in being there to nurture him and ensure that he did not suffer.

The Shift Begins

While having lunch with coworkers on a normal Tuesday in January 2011, I suddenly felt six quick stabs to my left temple and my eye began to water. Then my entire body experienced jolts of pain, numbness, tingling, and weakness moving from the top of my head through my face, down my arms, legs, and feet. I was fatigued and my balance was off. The left side of my face became numb and my mouth was drawn tightly to the right side. These episodes happened so often that I named it "my face thing."

In January 2014, I started experiencing recurrent, seizure-like symptoms that left me with no control of the movements in my hands, arms, and legs. At times, the weakness in my legs was so extreme that I became frozen and could not lift my feet or move my legs. These symptoms would improve after a period of time, only to randomly return again with no explanation.

For seven years doctors did their best to help me, but the limitations of traditional medicine could not explain what was wrong with me, much less offer a diagnosis or treatment. After a neurological study in April 2018, the neurologist suggested that my episodes could possibly be a result of a traumatic experience, perhaps from a past life. Finally, someone was speaking my language!

I was already practicing holistic approaches to wellness, so I knew in my heart that I had to be the one to take control of healing whatever was wrong with me. Since I had a prior interest in the NES Health bioenergetics program, I scheduled my first appointment with a local practitioner. This technology resonated with my understanding of the body's true control system, energetic flow, and how stress and emotional traumas trapped in the body can create physical effects that lead to disease. Thankfully, I experienced positive results with my own treatment protocols, leading me to invest in the NES Health Bioenergetics Practitioner course and establish my business, Evolved Holistic, so others could experience an alternative to traditional medicine.

The Guy Who Nudged Me

My high school sweetheart, who still holds a special and dear place in my heart, unexpectedly led me to my spiritual path. I heard a song on my car radio one Saturday morning in March 2012 that reminded me of him again, and, as fate or miracles happen, he contacted me the following Monday for the first time in twenty-five years. We communicated as if no time had passed; he admitted he thought of me often and that he was not currently in a happy place. He then shared a story about a "just for fun" psychic reading he had at a group event. The psychic accurately validated several specific

Chapter 18
My Healing Journey

details in his life and predicted that he would reunite with someone from his past. He was confident I was the one she was talking about. We wondered if our relationship was going to be renewed and if we were intended to be together. Although I was intrigued and excited at the possibility of this love reconnection, once again our lives unfolded in different directions. Apparently, I was not the one for him, and he was not the love of my life—not in this lifetime, anyway—yet there is no doubt in my heart that he came back into my life at the right time for a spiritual purpose.

I was in the process of exploring holistic health practices and was becoming more curious about spirituality and mediumship, so I listened to my heart and scheduled my first reading with a psychic medium. One of the first things that Spirit acknowledged was that it took a kick in my behind to get me there, i.e., "the nudge." That very first reading unveiled an inherent desire to immerse myself in my spiritual path. As a result of healing a part of my past and regaining my self-worth, I now felt at home, that I was where I belonged.

Getting to the Good

While launching my business Evolved Holistic, I participated in holistic expos in my area, where I connected with hypnotherapy and began exploring it for myself. My interest in hypnosis stemmed from an intuitive knowing there was still something from my childhood I needed to remember to further my healing. Perhaps, I thought, this was the cause of all the problems and issues I experienced in my life. I had acquired the knowledge, skills, and resources in my holistic toolbelt to manage and heal whatever it was. After all, at this point, how bad could it be? I simply wanted to reveal whatever it was so I could release it and move forward with peace in my life. Intuitively, I felt the call to complete the hypnotherapy practitioner course and include this service in my business, as I believed I needed to experience hypnotherapy for myself first in order to effectively help my clients.

My first hypnotherapy session focused on childhood regression to identify the blocks and feelings of emptiness in my life. The experience was emotional, insightful, and changed me in unexpected ways. The most surprising event that came up was not new or horrible, but rather something I had not realized about that childhood fall out of the window. Following hypnosis, I said to myself, "I already knew about the window incident and I have already forgiven my mother." What I would come to understand, however, was how that incident changed my world and formed my perspective of myself. It was the moment when I first learned to believe that I did not matter, and I had carried those thoughts and feelings of abandonment and unworthiness through all my life experiences. After that epiphany, my life, including certain relationships and situational patterns, began to make more sense. It helped transform my energy and allowed me to break the cycle of repeating unhealthy patterns.

I had subsequent hypnotherapy sessions, which helped me continue my journey to understanding and healing my childhood. During a recent session, I was taken to a time when I was ten years old and was a cheerleader for the local Pop Warner athletic league. The pivotal significance of this event was twofold: firstly, my mother was the team mom, so she was clearly there supporting me; secondly, it was a happy time when I felt like a normal kid, just like everyone else.

Truly Blessed and Grateful

Finding my spiritual path was my saving grace and the catalyst for positive transformation in my life. Primarily, I needed to remember that I am a child of God. Connecting with my higher spiritual self gave me trust, faith, and the evidence of life after death, validating the existence and power of Spirit communication and unconditional love. My church family and spiritual community provide the foundation for my spiritual understanding and intuitive development and is where I found guidance and support as I evolved from wounded to healed.

Chapter 18
My Healing Journey

To ensure my healing remains constant, I routinely incorporate Reiki, meditation, prayer, reflection, crystals, and other forms of self-love into my daily spiritual expression. My core belief is God's timing will provide what is intended for me *when* it is intended for me. This revelation teaches me patience and trust that everything happens for my highest and best good. When life becomes overwhelming or when I falter, I remember to use my resources to create a positive energy shift that brings me back to center.

I am truly blessed and grateful for the profound healing and inner peace that I now have, and for the discovery of my life purpose of being in service to others. It is my privilege to guide my clients on their journey to find their inner peace and heal their hearts and bodies from the effects of trauma and adverse experiences, so they too can evolve and embody their best self through energetic transformation.

ABOUT THE AUTHOR: Pamela Emmert, founder of Evolved Holistic, is a certified hypnotherapist, NES Health Bioenergetic Practitioner, Reiki Master Teacher, and spiritual intuitive. She connects with clients seeking a holistic approach to transformation, peace and comfort, and optimal health and wellness. Pamela is a practitioner at the Inner Wisdom Healing Center in Worthington, Ohio, and an active member of the National Association of Transpersonal Hypnotherapists, as well as the White Lily Chapel, a Spiritualist Church in Ashley, Ohio. She is a passionate supporter of charitable organizations and an advocate of individuals and families coping with early childhood traumas and those emerging from the cycle of domestic violence, addiction, homelessness, and incarceration.

Pamela Emmert
Evolved Holistic
evolvedholistic.com
pam@evolvedholistic.com
740-972-5206

CHAPTER 19

A Spiritual Scavenger Hunt

Millie America

Love has a way of messaging us from beyond the veil. Love is always around us, including from those who have passed on. We may hear the messages in songs, a story, or even signs in nature. Spirit will always find the way to communicate with us.

On March 14, 2023, one of the greatest loves of my life had his thirty-year death anniversary. I bought flowers and placed them on my altar for him. I had him with me all day. Truth be told, he has been with me since he died at the age of twenty-four. Christopher leaves me eleven cents a lot. I often find a dime and a penny in the most unusual places. That morning, I found them in a cup I pulled out of the kitchen cabinet. I hadn't used the cup in a while. When I grabbed it, I heard the change move, and there it was, eleven cents. I smiled and patted my heart while staring at the ceiling.

That week had been stressful. My little girl got lice at school and they spread to her younger brother, and I became obsessed with clearing it from them and sanitizing the entire house. That weekend, when they left for their father's home (as we share custody), I got busy cleaning and throwing stuff out.

Throughout the weekend I kept hearing the word "warrior" in shows and songs. I would see the word all over the place. Chris died in South Florida in 1993, and his body was flown to Warrior,

Alabama, to be buried near his mother. I kept asking my guides, out loud, why I needed to go to Warrior when I have him always nearby in spirit.

At 1:11 on Monday morning I was woken by someone in my room. The first word I heard was "Warrior." I looked up the distance between Warrior and Asheville, North Carolina, where I live. It was a little over six hours. I meditated that morning, Chris showed up in my meditation and, in his most loving manner, asked if I would go to his hometown soon.

The next day, without a plan, I got in my car at 5 a.m. and began driving over the mountains to Alabama. I have very little memory of things in my twenties due to a brain injury I sustained at thirty-three. I couldn't remember where Chris was buried, only that it was a Catholic church on some hill. What a crazy spiritual scavenger hunt this was becoming! During the drive, I spoke out loud to him and my angels. I asked for guidance. With every hour that brought me closer to that small town, my heart fluttered.

In the middle of nowhere, I spotted a McDonald's and stopped in for breakfast. I don't normally eat fast food, but there was nothing else around and I was starving. When my sausage McGriddle arrived, I opened it up to find just the pancakes and a sausage sandwiching them. I went to tell the cashier that they messed up my order. At that moment I realized that I'd gotten exactly what I asked for, even though I wanted eggs and cheese in it. I could almost hear Chris laughing and saying, "You have to be specific in life." I mumbled, "You should be more specific about why I am going to Warrior, Alabama."

After another thirty minutes of driving I arrived in the small town and googled the nearest Catholic church. It seemed to be the right place, at least that's what my vague recollection told me; however, when I parked my car and walked into the cemetery behind the church I couldn't remember where Chris was buried. It had been

Chapter 19
A Spiritual Scavenger Hunt

thirty years and during that time I was grieving him. The day of his funeral was basically a blur.

My oldest son called me while I was searching for the gravesite. I told him I was in Warrior, Alabama and he asked what I was doing there.

Good question!

"I was guided to come to Chris' old home," I replied, "I don't know why I am here. I can't remember his mother's last name. I have no clue how to explain this but I am supposed to be here."

That's when I saw it: the stone with Chris' name, and I burst into sobs. I had been so focused on finding the place that I hadn't given much thought to how I would feel when I got there. I asked my son to give me some time; I would communicate later. As I stood there, every emotion from grief to joy passed through me. The cold wind picked up and the giant tree behind me echoed sounds that broke me. I got on my knees, touching his headstone. I moved my fingers through his name and the dates. I stopped at the dash between the years.

"Your dash was so short," I said out loud. "I am sorry I haven't been here in decades. I figured you were always with me regardless of where I lived. Thank you for loving me so much. My life has been magical because you guided me, over and over, through the most difficult times. I love you. I don't know why you needed me to come. I don't remember your mother's name…"

I got up, wiping away the cold tears, then kissed the fingers on my right hand and placed them on the stone. Turning to leave, I realized I had no idea what else, if anything, I was to do in Warrior. About fifteen feet from Chris' gravesite, I almost tripped over a small plaque on the ground. I looked at it and saw there was just one word: his mother's last name.

I sprinted to the car to look up her name, see if she still lived in Warrior, or was alive at all. When she showed up without an address,

I decided to go to their city hall and get information. The chief of the fire department helped, giving me two possible addresses in this small town. The woman at the first house told me that Chris' mom didn't live there anymore. I drove up the road to the second address—a beautiful country home about a half-acre back from the street and gated. I sat in the front of the gate for about twenty minutes before a woman and five huge dogs approached. She was kind. I asked if she knew where Chris' mother lived, she told me she had bought the house from her five years earlier. Then she sent me up the road yet again.

My stomach was in knots. I felt sick. How was I to show up at a stranger's door after thirty years? She was now in her eighties—what if she had dementia and didn't even remember me? As I pulled to a stop in the driveway, I felt a hand grab mine on the steering wheel. I had to get a hold of my emotions.

I knocked on the door. An elderly woman in a walker opened. I recognized her.

"Hi! My name is Millie. I was friends with your son many years ago in the power transmission place…"

"Of course I remember you," she exclaimed. "Oh, you were the love of his life!" She stepped forward and pulled me into a hug. I began to cry.

"What are you doing here? You know his death anniversary was last week. It's been thirty years."

"I know," I replied, holding her hand in mine. "That's why I am here."

"You drove all the way from Miami today?"

"No, I live in Asheville now."

We shared more small details, including the fact that she had had a stroke a few months earlier; that's why she had the walker. Then she again asked why I had come. I told her I really didn't know, only that I had to come today.

Chapter 19
A Spiritual Scavenger Hunt

"You know, last week I was sitting here praying to Chris. I told him I no longer felt him, but if he could hear me, could he please send an angel to my door so I know he's listening. And, here you are, Millie!" Her eyes had puddles of water ready to release. I knew she was in the middle of her physical therapy session, as the practitioner was waiting on her.

"I am no angel," I told her, "but your son has a way of making sure you know he's with you always."

We hugged and said our goodbyes. I didn't ask for her number. She didn't either. It was meant as closure for her and a deep awareness that her son was always with her. I am a mother of eight children. Losing a child has to be the hardest thing for any parent.

Chris was young, handsome, intelligent, and had a beautiful life ahead of him. The week that he died, he asked me to marry him. We were both in other relationships. I had gone on a trip with my boyfriend and broke up with him. Chris was coming back from breaking up with his girlfriend when his car hit a wall on I-95. He was killed instantly and found with a small Spanish/English dictionary clutched in his hand.

Chris knew he would die young. He had experienced two near-deaths in his life. We spoke a lot about them and how they had changed his life. One night, while lying in bed, he turned over and asked me to please wear a particular dress to his funeral. He always loved it when I wore it to work. I told him it would definitely not look good on me when we were old. Something in him was preparing him for his next journey.

After leaving his mother's house, I immediately began the six-hour drive so I could make it home before dark. While sitting in a horrible traffic jam in Chattanooga, Tennessee, I said out loud, "I am glad your mom got her message. I miss you. Today I have missed you more than I have in a very long time. But now that I got this done for you (I giggled), could you please help me out on those two things I keep asking from God and the angels? What am I supposed to be doing with my life, Chris?"

Suddenly, the Spanish music I had been listening to on Spotify changed, mid-song, to an English song. The lyrics were answering my question. I began to sob. Thank goodness we were at a standstill. I sat there shaking my head, tears running down my face, snot everywhere. I whispered through the painful release, "Thank you, darling. I love you, then, now, and forever."

Listening to Spirit is how I live my life. This is one of the things I help my clients do. Everyone wants to know how to listen. It's not easy because we've been programmed to listen to our egos. The art of listening to our intuition is not always accessible with the daily demands of this modern world.

About a year ago, I began working with an incredible woman who owned several restaurants and other businesses. Her wealth was wonderful but something was missing in her life; she wanted a more spiritual connection. She was a multitasker doing a million things at once, and her ego was constantly in the way, making it hard to sit and listen to her intuition. She had been to several retreats in South America prior to us meeting. She felt that Spirit was trying to communicate with her on a deeper level.

We met each week and, little by little, were able to disconnect from ego and start connecting to Spirit. She felt that she was finally being guided in her journey. She sold one of her businesses and started to shift the old beliefs. She began to meditate every single morning. Stopping the busyness and stepping into the silence was pivotal. These days, her life is completely different. She is softer, less prone to outbursts. She can step into the 3D world with exceptional faith and she trusts without having to overanalyze every situation in her life.

The only thing that changed was her beliefs and willingness to listen to something other than herself. She is one badass warrior!

Chapter 19
A Spiritual Scavenger Hunt

Her heart has been opened to receive guidance. Her life has now become one giant spiritual scavenger hunt. What a joy and honor to work with her to assist and witness her incredible transformation.

Whether you know it or not, you are a badass warrior too. You conquer things every single day. Many times, you don't want to. You avoid them and then you have to tackle them with the same ferocity as a Celtic Warrior Goddess fighting to stay alive. These experiences are what make us spiritual beings having human experiences.

It's about love. Those messages are always about love because they come from a loved one. Your angels and spirit guides are always there, helping you evolve and raise your frequency with small reminders that only you can decipher.

I trust. I learn. I love. I forgive. I believe. That is all I am here to do. The rest is up to God and His messengers. How about you? Do you know when your next scavenger hunt is going to remind you that you are a Spiritual Warrior in a world that needs you always?

ABOUT THE AUTHOR: Millie America is a sought-after gifted medium and psychic whose readings and counseling sessions help others unlock their spiritual gifts and find their authenticity. She is the founder of Sacred Journey Inward, a daily blog and social media phenomenon where she lifts others through compelling and motivational stories. A metaphysical facilitator, empath, and cheerleader of love, she helps people find what is lost and remember what was. She is an Amazon best-selling author for her spiritual memoir, *Erasable* and her collaboration in *U Empath You*. Millie is driven to help others fulfill their potential and purpose.

Millie America
sacredjourneyinward.com
sacredjourneyinward@gmail.com
828-707-8897

CHAPTER 20

Journey of the Heart

Linda Stansberry

I love hindsight. When I look back on challenging life events, I see how synchronistically these events are orchestrated. Viewing adversity postmortem, with a different set of eyes, it is easy to see all the intricately designed details surrounding a hardship's unfoldment.

2013 was my "lost year," as I spent it working through stage-three colon cancer. I was three weeks shy of my forty-ninth birthday when, at my annual physical, my primary care doctor pushed me (again) to get a colonoscopy because of my family history. He had directed me to get one at forty-seven, then insisted at forty-eight. I had continued to hold out, as I was planning to wait until I turned fifty. This time, bless his heart (and I mean this in the good way, not in the Southern "fuck you, buddy" kind of way), he literally took my hand, walked me to the receptionist, and made me an appointment to see the gastroenterologist. I was taken aback that he was so adamant, so, instead of waiting until fifty as I had planned, I accepted the appointment.

The six or so polyps taken during that first colonoscopy *looked* benign, but one polyp came back showing cancer. As a precaution, I had nine inches removed on either side of where the cancerous polyp was found, along with a dozen lymph nodes. Again, visually they looked fine. However, three of those lymph nodes came back with cancer cells. I was literally diagnosed at the earliest possible moment with a late-stage cancer. This all may sound horrible at first blush, but this is really the big, beautiful Holy-WOW-God-moment you only see with hindsight. Can you see how miraculously this all unfolded?

A few days later, I was sitting in an oncologist's office. I never imagined I'd hear the words, "You have stage-three colon cancer." Now that I had, I would soon begin the process of healing my physical vessel by poisoning it with chemo. Makes perfect sense, right? I made the best decision I could based on what I knew at that time in my life. The only thing on my mind at that point was living to see my children's children and spending as much time with the love of my life, with whom I had just reunited two years prior. My Gregory.

My Heart's Journey

Greg was my high school sweetheart. We had a tumultuous on-again, off-again romance from ages sixteen to twenty. I was all about the "on again" parts, but I would inevitably exhaust my welcome with this young boy who preferred the "off again" parts. Greg liked the *idea* of a girlfriend, but really wanted to spend his free time partying with his buddies. Yet, we had a deep and undeniable connection because of our similar upbringings. We were both raised as feral children, navigating our world with single moms who rarely knew or seemed concerned about where we were and who we were with.

I remember being so excited to attend senior prom with Greg. We were usually (and conveniently) broken up during school dances—in fact, I can count on one finger the times he attended one with me. Sure enough, two weeks before prom, Greg and I were off again.

Chapter 20
Journey of the Heart

But, in true fashion, we really couldn't stay away from each other very long.

Greg reached out to me the night of my school's All Night Grad Party. He asked to meet outside my place. I remember looking from our second-story window, seeing him leaning against the hood of his car. It was like a scene from the movie *Say Anything*, except he didn't have a boom box. I was so excited yet still so damn pissed off at him at the same time. I was tired of our on-and off-agains. I didn't know what would get through to him, so I said, "Greg, no one will ever love you the way that I can love you." That line hit him straight in the heart.

When I look back on that one spoken line, I can feel the entire cosmos rush into my heart, as if in that one single second my soul is born all over again. My heart expands with a knowing as deep as the Grand Canyon. All the sensations of that moment poured over me—the colors, the smells, the feeling I felt as I said those words. Words whispered directly from my heart.

After high school, I moved to Colorado for college, eventually landing a gig at a TV station which allowed me to drop out. Greg and I made a valiant attempt to keep a long distance relationship going, but it was futile. He soon decided to join the Navy. I, being anti-establishment, was very unhappy with that decision. We were off again.

A few times Greg called me from basic training, drunk. One of those calls consisted of him belittling my TV career. That didn't go over well.

Then, after basic training, Greg decided to visit me in Wichita, where I had moved for a better job. I was still angry at his drunk comments about my career and far from forgiveness. I gave him a sub-zero cold shoulder. I am amazed he put up with my shit. He stayed the whole long, miserable weekend at my place, sleeping on the floor and being snubbed by me.

We never spoke again after that.

Later, I met someone in Kansas and eventually married. Shortly after Greg found out, he married his friend in Charleston. We ended up having our first children a week apart. Interesting how the matrix plays out sometimes.

Thirty Years Later

Once the internet was born, I would occasionally search for him online. I was never able to locate him. When Facebook was born, I figured I would find him. Instead, I found his sister, who, sadly, had no Greg on her friends list.

Then one day the stars aligned. I hopped on Facebook and saw a notification: "comment from Greg Stansberry" underneath a comment I'd made on his sister's photo.

The hook was set instantly, for both of us. We started messaging, then talking, catching up on each others' lives. I was now living in Florida and six months into an eighteen-month divorce. He was staring at his soon-to-be empty nest and his partner, with whom he had nothing in common.

One day I asked him why he showed up in Wichita knowing I was so mad at him. He said he was hoping I would follow him off to the Navy in Charleston. I might have, too, if only *he had asked*. We rode the wagon of regret for a couple of years until we both came to the conclusion that we had to learn lessons from our previous relationships so we would know what we wanted from our relationship together.

After Greg and I committed to each other, he left his teaching job in Tennessee and moved in. He had a chunk of money from his retirement fund and was looking for a new career.

One night, over a bottle of wine, I asked, "If you could do

Chapter 20
Journey of the Heart

anything that you wanted to, what would you choose?"

He didn't hesitate. "Be a pilot."

I wanted that dream for him. I said I would support him through this career change and he could use all his money and begin what he calls his "retirement job" at age forty-five.

I was flying high! The boy I'd fallen in love with all those years ago was back in my life. He had transformed into a deeply good, kind, and loving man. It was Greg & Linda 2.0.

Cancer's Gift

My colon cancer journey taught me deep gratitude and to trust my gut (pun intended). Cancer made me examine the uncharted territory deep in my soul. I was exploring my inner world, digging into my own psyche, journaling my feelings, reading books on manifesting, psychics, and intuition. I was expressing my inner spirit through artwork and beginning a meditation practice during my nature walks. Cancer led me on an expedition of heart expansion.

I viewed all aspects of my life through a different lens. I was starting to see the overlay of the matrix before I ever knew that was a thing. I had a ten-thousand-foot view while planted firmly on the ground.

Crash Landing

In 2013 Greg became a flight instructor. He was now three years into flying. Being that I ran the Creative Department at a local news station, I would joke with him that he needed to always answer my calls, no matter what, in case I heard about a small plane crash on our news.

On August 1, 2014, Greg crash-landed a Cessna 172RG outside of Apalachicola, in the marsh on the edge of the Gulf of Mexico.

Greg's work sent him to Apalchicola to pick up a plane that had broken down and was now allegedly repaired. Shortly after take-off the engine died. He was barely getting enough lift and headed toward a bank of trees at the end of the runway. Somehow he got the engine started, but a minute later it died, again, this time as he was climbing to clear power lines. Miraculously, he got the engine started a third time. And then a fourth. As he got it started again, he knew he'd need to put the plane down in the Gulf if it died a fifth time. As you can guess, this is exactly what happened. Greg saw some sawgrass ahead and dropped the plane in the marsh.

I will never forget my utter shock when I received a phone call from him telling me about it. There I was, not even a year past my last chemo treatment, and the love of my life was in a plane crash!

With each setback and each trauma, the events that can break us could ultimately make us, if we choose. I am a warrior. My battle wounds are a badge of honor. Hindsight showed me that this was actually not a setback at all, but yet another golden brick on the road to uncovering what we are made of. Greg and I both witnessed firsthand the fragility of life. Near-death experiences are powerful reminders to embrace every moment and every loved one. Live for the day and do only what lights us up. The rest doesn't matter.

Spiritual Immersion 101

My last treatment was October 7, 2013. I returned to work a month later. My cancer year really opened my eyes to the toxic cesspool that was my career. To save my health and sanity, Greg generously offered to return the favor and now support me as I started a new career path.

I opened my own photography business in 2015. I had finally come full circle. Photography was what I'd originally wanted after high school; however, my Mom convinced me that it wasn't a "real job." Now, here I was, starting again at fifty-one.

Chapter 20
Journey of the Heart

I immersed myself in getting my business off the ground. At the same time, I now had the capacity to listen to the soft heart whispers that were there to guide me. I finally had the space to be present in my life.

Plus, the more heart-expanding moments I experienced, the farther I was drawn into my spiritual studies. My spiritual practices helped me to realize that I wasn't a victim of my circumstances. Awful things did not happen to me, they happened for me, allowing my soul to learn, expand, and grow. I received hundreds of large and small lessons, probably the biggest of which was focusing on myself and doing the inner work. From there, everything else would fall into place.

My everyday life felt lighter. My smiles, frequent. My heart, swollen with gratitude. I was shifting my inner world and my outer world was coming up to match that vibration.

Take Me or Leave Me

I was soon guided to start my own spiritual practice. I began sharing sessions with friends to hone my abilities. I was super excited, however, I was seriously worried what Greg would think. Sure, he was aware of my woo-woo side, but he really had no idea the depths of what was unfolding for me. I was afraid to bare my soul.

The worry was awful, my heart felt constricted like it was in a vice. I had to do something. I told myself, "If Greg truly is the love of my life, he will accept me for who I am and who I am becoming. If he doesn't, then I guess our relationship has run its course."

I slowly started opening up about my experiences. Sharing stories and what I learned. Talking about more and more "woo-woo" topics. That free, expansive feeling started coming back. I was focusing on me, not him or our relationship. I was being true to myself, my soul. From there, our relationship had the freedom to flourish.

I am enjoying my cancer-free journey on this wild rollercoaster of life, following where my heart leads me and looking forward to the lessons that lay ahead.

ABOUT THE AUTHOR: Linda Stansberry is an Intuitive Creative Alchemist, professional photographer, blogger, and published author. Her blog, *Finding Zen with Cancer,* serves as the launch pad to her first book of the same name. She's a spiritual practitioner, offering intuitive and psychic readings, quantum guidance, and channeled messages, plus Soul Dragon Art and Readings, Soul Portraits, and much more. She is soon to release her first Oracle Card Deck, *SoulScripts*. Her acclaimed podcast, *Conversation for the Soul,* is broadcast on multiple platforms, including YouTube and her website, TheOwlandTheCrone.com.

Linda Stansberry
TheOwlandTheCrone@gmail.com
727-403-5516
TheOwlandTheCrone.com
LindaStansberryPhotography.com

About the Authors

**Are you inspired by the stories in this book?
Let the authors know.**

See the contact information at the end of each chapter and reach out to them.

They'd love to hear from you!

Author Rights & Disclaimer

Each author in this book retains the copyright and all inherent rights to their individual chapter. Their stories are printed herein with each author's permission.

Each author is responsible for the individual opinions expressed through their words. Powerful You! Publishing bears no responsibility for the content of the stories by these authors.

Acknowledgments & Gratitude

To the beautiful authors of this book, we respect, appreciate, and love you. You've stepped forward to shine your light through your stories and you have done so with beauty, grace, and courage. As your words show, you are strong, determined, resilient, gentle, and open. You provide a beautiful example for those facing challenges, and we're truly honored to share this journey with you. We thank you for stepping forth so that others may learn from you. You are each a beautiful symbol for a life lived from the heart & soul.

Our editor Dana Micheli: Your intuition, sense of humor, creativity, and willingness are a perfect fit to get to the heart of the stories. We appreciate our partnership and friendship, and we love you.

Our training team: AmondaRose Igoe, Kathy Sipple, Karen Flaherty, Francine Sinclair, and Melanie Herschorn—your expertise, big hearts, and guidance are so helpful for our authors. We appreciate each of you.

Carol Collins: We are honored to be in this sandbox with you. We are grateful for your gifts, insights, and willingness to spread positivity and Divine wisdom that assists individuals on our shared journey.

We are forever grateful for the many beautiful and loving individuals who grace our lives—friends, family, colleagues, our tribe. We're grateful for each of you and for the gifts you generously offer.

Above all, we are grateful for the Divine Spirit that flows through us each day providing continued blessings, lessons, and opportunities for growth, peace, and JOY!

Namaste` and Blessings, Love and Gratitude,
Sue Urda and Kathy Fyler
Publishers

About Sue Urda and Kathy Fyler

Sue and Kathy have been business partners since 1994. They have received many awards and accolades for their businesses over the years and continue to they love the work they do and the people they attract to work with. As publishers, they are honored to help people share their stories, passions, and lessons.

Their mission is to raise the vibration of people and the planet and to connect and empower women in their lives. Their calling has been years in the making 'forever' and is a gift from Spirit.

The strength of their partnership lies in their deep respect, love, and understanding of one another as well as their complementary skills and knowledge. Kathy is a technology enthusiast, web goddess, and freethinker. Sue is an author and speaker with a love of creative undertakings and great conversations. Their honor, love, and admiration for each other are boundless.

Together their energies combine to feed the flames of countless women who are seeking truth, empowerment, joy, peace, and connection with themselves, their own spirits, and other women. They believe we are all here in this lifetime to support and love of one another, and they are grateful to fulfill this purpose through their publishing company.

Connect with Sue and Kathy:

Powerful You! Publishing
powerfulyoupublishing.com
goodvibesgals.com
sueurda.com

About Carol Collins

Carol Collins is a gifted alpha-state channeler for the Jeshua Collective. Through her, Jeshua teaches The Essential Material—collective consciousness, manifesting with ease, health and wellness through natural healing, and intuitive advancement—what they call the Four Pillars of Learning. Jeshua dictated 11 books in 2021, her second year of channeling, and currently has many more in the queue for publishing.

Jeshua is revolutionizing intuitive training and clearing the pathway to a true, clear, verbal connection with nonphysical Beings. They describe their work through Carol as "the depth of Edgar Cayce, the substance of Jane Roberts, in the style of Esther Hicks." Carol has been interviewed by celebrity personalities, featured in over two dozen magazines, was named to several Top 10 Women to Watch Lists, and is internationally known for giving powerfully accurate readings. Carol is rising swiftly to be among the great channelers bringing true, eloquent Teaching from

To contact her please visit the website at:
>thepittsburghmedium.com

Follow and subscribe to her social media channels:
>Instagram: The Pittsburgh Medium
>YouTube: The Pittsburgh Medium
>Twitter: @pitsbrghmedium
>Facebook: The Pittsburgh Medium
>Facebook Fan Page: The Teachings of Jeshua
>TikTok: The Pittsburgh Medium
>Peloton: @eatlovebike

Powerful You! Publishing

Sharing Wisdom ~ Shining Light

Are You Called to Be an Author?

If you're like most people, you may find the prospect of writing a book daunting. Where to begin? How to proceed? No worries! We're here to help.

Whether you choose to contribute to an anthology or write your own book, we're here for you. We'll be your guiding light, professional consultant, and enthusiastic supporter. If you see yourself as an author partnering with a publishing company that has your best interest at heart and expertise to back it up, we'd be honored to be your publisher.

We provide personalized guidance through the writing and editing process, as well as many necessary tools for your success as an author. We offer complete publishing packages and our service is designed for a personal and optimal author experience.

We are committed to helping individuals express their voice and shine their light into the world. Are you ready to start your journey as an author? Do it with Powerful You! Publishing.

Powerful You! PUBLISHING
Sharing Wisdom ~ Shining Light

Powerful You! Publishing
239-280-0111
powerfulyoupublishing.com

Collaboration Books

Empowering Transformations for Women
Women Living Consciously
Journey to Joy
Pathways to Vibrant Health & Well-Being
Women Living Consciously Book II
Healthy, Abundant, and Wise
Keys to Conscious Business Growth
The Gifts of Grace & Gratitude
Heal Thy Self
Empower Your Life
Heart & Soul
The Beauty of Authenticity
WOKE
The Art and Truth of Transformation for Women
Women Living On Purpose
U Empath You
Women Living In Alignment

GUIDED...

It's the Feeling You Get When You *Know*.

**Listen to Your Heart.
Follow Your Innate Wisdom.**